Break Every Chain

Cheyenne Bostock

Break Every Chain

(Lesson Every Father Should Teach His Son About Life, Love & Relationships)

Author: Cheyenne Bostock

Copyright © 2014 AskCheyB

All rights reserved. No part of this publication may be reproduced, distributed, or Transmitted in any form or by any means, or stored in a database or retrieval system, without the prior permission of the publisher.

This book is writrten as a source of motivation and inspiration. The contents of this Book has been carefully researched in efforts to ensure accuracy. The author and publisher assume no responsibility for any losses, damages, or injuries incurred as a result of applying the information provided in this book.

AskCheyB P.O. Box 380846

Brooklyn, NY 11238

Visit our website at www.askcheyb.com Follow @AskCheyB

Library of Congress Cataloging-in-Publication Data is available upon request.

ISBN: 978-0988425835

Printed in the United States of America

Photography by @HottShotzPhotos www.hottshotzphotos.com

Printing December 2014 10 9 8 7 6 5 4 3 2 1

Dedication

This book is dedicated to my son Ethan and also to all the men who are striving to become better brothers, fathers, husbands and friends. I hope this book gives you the tools you need to become the best men you can possibly be.

CONTENTS

Introduction 1
Chapter 1: What It Means To Be A Man 3
              Manhood 5
              Brotherhood 10
              Be A Man Of Integrity 18
              Be Confident 24
              Respect Yourself 30
              Respect Women 36
Chapter 2: The Learning Curve 43
              Learn How To Be Responsible 45
              Learn How To Manage Money 51
              Learn How To Listen 57
              Learn How To Share 63
              Learn How To Dress 69
              Learn How To Cook 75
Chapter 3: Understanding A Woman 83
              Know The Value Of A Woman 85
              Women Love To Talk 91
              A Woman Will Submit To You When You Submit To God 97
              A Woman Needs Romance 103
              A Woman Wants A Man With A Plan 110
              A Woman Doesn't Like To Share Her Man 116
Chapter 4: Courtship 123
              Friendship Is The Key To Romance 125

  Be A Gentlemen 131
  Take Your Lady Out 137
  Know Your Worth 143
  Show Your Worth 149
  Be Creative 155
Chapter 5: Commitment 161
  The Power Of Monogamy 163
  Introduce Her To Your Family & Friends 171
  Marriage Is A Full-Time Job 177
  If You Love Her, Put A Ring On It 183
  Marriage Is An Upgrade 188
  Til Death Do You Part 195
Chapter 6: Fatherhood 201
  Get Ready To Be A Father 203
  Plan To Be A Better Father 210
  Be A Good Step Dad 215
  Discipline Your Child 221
  Spend Quality Time With Your Children . 228
  Support Your Child 234
50 Motivational Quotes From Cheyenne Bostock 241
Bio 247

Introduction

There are countless references for women to turn to when it comes to advice on life and relationships; books, magazines, TV, blogs, and more, mainly because experts target the people who spend money on these areas of interest. However we *all* need improvement in our relationships, our finances and in our walk in life. As men, we don't always express in words what we are going through or that we need help, but our lack of expression is simply the mask we put on as to not appear weak in front of our peers. For many young men, there is a lack of a father figure in the household, so the lessons on how to be a man are often provided by the mother.

Often times the mother *herself* is still trying to figure out men, let alone try to teach her son how to be one. A fatherless son will go years without knowing how to be financially independent and responsible, or how to properly approach a lady, or how to tie a tie and dress up for an occasion. These patterns not only last in the young man's life, but it moves onto the next generation as he will more than likely teach the few lessons that he's been able to learn for himself *if* he's man enough to stick around and handle his responsibilities like a man. Fear of not knowing what to do or how to do it prevents a lot of men from taking accountability for their actions and owning up to their responsibilities.

In this book, men will receive valuable insight on how to break the chains that restrict them from being upstanding, quality men of substance not only for themselves, but also for their relationships and their communities. As a father, I pride myself in raising my son to be better than I am, and fully functional without me so that he can make this world a better place. I didn't have the luxury of having my biological father raise me, yet and still I decided that I didn't want to be a statistic and that I will break every chain that held me back from getting more out of life. I hope my son and all who read this book would make the choice to break every chain too.

Chapter 1:

What It Means To Be A Man

Manhood

Often times when a male figure is lacking in strength, courage and/or wisdom you'll hear a person shout "Be a man!". They say this because as a man, society holds us to a higher standard, a standard that requires us to possess great leadership skills, discernment, and a sense of fearlessness. Yes, we are all human, we make mistakes, we fall short, we grow weary, and we certainly don't have the power to know it all, but as men, it's our responsibility to come up with a plan to try and figure things out against any and all odds. It goes back to principles. If you base everything you do in life on principles and stay focused on those principles, you will achieve progressive results in every aspect of your life.

Every man has the ability to lead, we simply have to believe in ourselves, swallow our pride and let go of fear so that we can be effective in our leadership. There's nothing wrong with falling, just so long as you get back up, learn from your mistakes and try again. People will respect your more for attempting to do something great, rather than attempting to do nothing at all. Fear, pride and ego can hold you back from achieving the impossible if you let it, but once you learn to overcome it, you will reach unbelievable new heights. Once you have a plan for the level of success you want to reach, you will be well on your way.

Take for example a man's desire to get close to a woman. You'll first have to plan your approach based on a number of different factors: Her mood, surroundings, body language, etc. After figuring out the best way to approach her, you then have to figure out a way to conclude what she is missing from her life and how you will add value to her life. After you've succeeding in getting her attention, you then have to plan the next steps for keeping her attention. For the average man, this process is like clockwork, and after years of practice, one may even become an expert at picking up women. Success at picking up women can be fun, but rest assured there is so much more to life, and you can achieve so much more in other areas of your life if you applied the same hard work, dedication and discipline used in picking up women for example.

Take for example a job opportunity. To increase your chances at landing an interview and getting hired, you would first research the company, figure out what positions are available, come up with a creative resume and cover letter specifically geared towards that particular company, apply for the job, follow up, and then make a great impression during the interview. It's not hard to do, you simply have to want it badly enough to not allow anything to get in your way. By disciplining yourself and focusing on your goals, it's possible to achieve anything. If you allow yourself to get distracted by things that don't add value to your life, you'll be taking value away from your life and the people who have grown to depend on you.

Being a man isn't about your age, how much facial hair you have, how deep your voice is or how effortlessly you could strong arm someone. Being a man is about maturity, growth, and being a responsible and fully functional member of society. It means that you have integrity and you treat yourself and others with dignity and respect, you pay your bills on time, you are stable both emotionally and spiritually and constantly working to improve yourself. It's a lot of work to be successful in all areas of your life, but it's indeed worth it. Being successful in one area will give you the confidence and motivation to aspire to be successful in all others.

Happiness is about how well you can balance the many challenges you will face in life. Throughout the course of your life, you will experience good times, bad times, ups, downs and complete turnarounds, and you need to be ready for it. The first step to accomplishing this is to connect on a spiritual level to a higher power, submitting to that power, and then allowing that power to influence every aspect of your life. Having a positive and optimistic outlook on life will help you to overcome any and every obstacle in your life, and it will also rub off on other people. When people see that you are full of joy and happiness through all you're going through, you'll give them hope, and for this reason they will want to remain closely associated with you.

It's particularly important for a *man* to figure out his purpose in life because we are expected to lead. No one (man or woman) who knows their worth wants to follow behind a man who is financially irresponsible, emotionally unstable, or spiritually lost. But once you finally walk in your purpose and shine the light that has always been inside of you, you will begin to see the trust amongst your family members and friends regained, relationships repaired and rebuilt, and hope once again restored. It's one thing for a person to not trust you, it's another for you to not be trustworthy. People want to see you do well, but they can't achieve success for you and are waiting for you to believe in yourself and show them through actions how your belief system has driven you to prosperity. Only then will they opt to follow your proven path of leadership.

Even after you have achieved personal success, it's important then for you to aspire for something greater. Never grow complacent, for once you stop working towards being better, doing better and having better, the people around you will no longer look to you for that glimmer of hope that shined when you once climbed mountains, broke barriers and achieved the impossible. As a man, you should look to be great and inspire greatness in those around you. That is what leadership is all about; showing others how it's done, being fearless, having faith, being open to ideas and executing them to the best of your ability.

A man without a plan will never achieve long-term success with a woman of substance because ultimately she wants to be led into prosperity. It's easy to lead a woman who lacks substance astray because she hasn't yet figured out what her value as a woman is, or what value you as a man should bring to the table. Going after women who don't know their worth is like challenging a child in an arm wrestling match. Sure you'll win the fight, but there's no glory in it, there's no pride, and there's certainly no greater sense of accomplishment because the goals you've set for yourself weren't high enough. There is greater value in knowing who you are, where you're going, and who you want to take with you than wasting valuable time at pit stops along the road to success.

Achieving short-term success with a woman who lacks substance takes away from the time you could be spending building yourself up to become the quality man of substance you were destined to be. No matter what quality of women you're attracting now, once you've become the best man you can possibly be, you'll attract the best possible woman. When you finally grow into your manhood, you'll develop not only physically, but also financially, spiritually and emotionally. Attracting a more quality woman however is only one of the many perks that comes with being a quality man of substance. Your relationship with other men will be strengthened because they now admire your discipline, your drive, and your determination; they value your leadership. You'll have respect amongst your peers.

Setting higher goals for yourself and achieving them will help you to further see your value, and allow others to also see the value in you. Consider yourself a diamond in the rough; instead of covering yourself up with things that hide who you are and who you are destined to be, take the time dust yourself off so that you can see yourself shine, build up your confidence/esteem so that when you step out into the world, you not only know your worth, but you show your worth. Knowing what your value as a man will be the key that unlocks the doors to job opportunities, a closer relationship with your friends/family members, a life of prosperity with a quality woman of substance, but most of all peace of mind within yourself.

Brotherhood

I'm the second youngest of 5 boys and 1 girl born to my mother, and I'm thankful to have had so many male influences in my life growing up. No matter what, I've always had someone to talk to, engage with and get valuable insight from. Whenever my brothers wanted to go somewhere, my mother would tell them "take your brother Cheyenne with you". Maybe she wanted the house completely vacant so that she could spend time alone with her husband (my step-father) but I'd like to think she primarily wanted my brothers and I to spend more quality time together. ☺

Two of my older brothers Travis and Shane hated taking me with them because they were one year and 3 years older than I was and they wanted to do what older kids did. I on the other hand simply wanted to spend quality time with my brothers. They were good looking, talented, ambitious and all the girls in the neighborhood wanted to know them. No matter where we lived (New York, New Jersey, Atlanta, or Texas) popularity followed them. My eldest brother Milton seemed like the King of Brooklyn, everyone knew who he was (it seemed) and it felt good knowing that people acknowledged and respected him.

Me, I was the smart, funny, athletic, proper speaking cute kid that everyone referred to as "the little brother". Always associated with my brothers' reputation in the neighborhood. During the early stages of my childhood, I would create my own circle of friends, but still found joy in being invited to hang out with my older brothers and their friends. It made me feel as though my brothers were proud to be my brothers, proud to have me around, and proud to introduce me to their network of friends. I would stay as silent as possible to prove that I was able to handle being in such a privileged position and to ensure that I would be invited again.

My mother had her reasons for having me tag along with my older siblings. She wanted to know where they were going, what they were doing and whom they were doing it with. She counted on me for this sort of information, and I was always sure to deliver. That might explain why my older siblings didn't want me around. lol. I respected my brothers and I admired them a lot, and I cared enough about them to let an adult (my mom) know anytime I felt they were doing things that would stir up trouble for themselves and for us as a family.

My brothers were my protection; I wasn't big enough, strong enough or tough enough to stand my own ground at the time. Meanwhile, no one in the neighborhood would dare cross my older brothers. Anytime I had a problem with someone, I would simply name drop one of my brothers and if that didn't work, I would run and tell my older brothers that there was a problem and they would see to it that it was fixed. My brothers taught me how to defend myself, how to stand up for myself, and how to let no one take away my dignity.

If you can imagine growing up in a house full of boys, you already know there were many physical altercations. Someone is always trying to gain control over something (i.e. Food, a spot on the couch, the remote control, etc). If there wasn't a woman around to mediate, then there would more than likely be a yelling match, followed swiftly by a wrestling and/or boxing match. I was no match for any of my older brothers, but I didn't back down, and then on top of that I'd be the first to tell my mom that I was being picked on when she got home. Since I was normally the honest one of the bunch, my word had more credibility than theirs and my mom would always come to my rescue.

Negotiating, debating and fighting with my brothers hurt me at the time, but it helped build my character. Facing my brothers, men who I admire and respect was one of the most difficult things in the world to do. Now that it's behind me, I can confidently defend myself against any adversary. When we fought against each other, we did so because we didn't know how to talk to one another as brothers. We looked at one another as competition as opposed to teammates.

My older brother Shane and Travis, who were closer in age fought all the time, and yet they hung out all the time as well. It was clear that they loved each other; they just didn't know how to show it. As we grow and mature, we learn more about ourselves, which opens up the door for love and understanding. People who are not open to listening and learning more about other people's feelings often spend countless hours trying to get people to understand theirs. In a brotherhood, respect for one another's thoughts and feelings are essential to the success of that relationship.

My eldest brother Milton moved out of the house before I could even remember, which made his visits so much more exciting! Sometimes my mom would give us a heads up on when he was coming to stay with us for the weekend, and sometimes she would let it be a surprise. Milton is tall (6'2), always well dressed in the latest fashion and was an excellent basketball player. Forget Michael Jordan, we wanted to be like our big brother Milton Bostock. If we were outside playing and saw him coming down the street, we would run like wild maniacs to greet him while yelling "MILTON!!!!!!"

Why were we so happy to see him? Because we missed him, we enjoyed our fellowship with our brother and we needed the connection. We needed those special moments where he took us to the park for a few hours to play, took us to the movies, or simply treated us to a soda, chips or some candy at the store. If you add up the dollar amount that it took for our big brother to make us happy, it wouldn't amount to much. The true value is the time he took to come back home and spend quality time with his little brothers.

As men, we hardly ever express to other men how we truly feel about them. Once we swallow our pride and express to our brothers that we love them, we appreciate them, and that we want to have them around, the stronger the bond will be. Often times we disregard men's feelings because we assume that they'll figure out a way to get past their hurt and pain on their own, or with the help of a woman. In a brotherhood, you take care of not only your sisters, but also your brothers. A strong man can build a solid kingdom, so we must continue to encourage our brothers, empower our brothers, and work together.

Right when I started high school, two of my older brothers were incarcerated right around the same time, which left me and my youngest brother Joshua behind. I had just moved to Dallas, Texas with my sister Jordi and my parents soon moved to Texas as well. I was in a new place literally and figuratively, I didn't know anyone, I had no one to protect me, and I was a New Yorker living in Texas. It was my turn to be *the* big brother and protect my younger brother, as well as show him the ropes.

I took great pride in it because Joshua looked up to me, he respected me and he was counting on me. I was tough on him, the way my older brothers were tough on me, but at the end of the day, it was all out of love. Our relationship wasn't perfect, but there was a lesson in everything that we did. Joshua and I are 4 years apart and we've shared a room at almost every place we've lived so I had the greatest advantage over all of our siblings to connect with him. I would come home and see him playing video games and I would ask, "Did you finish your homework?" and of course he would always say, "Yes".

I could've trusted that he was telling me the truth, but I'm much older and wiser and I used to pull those same tricks as well. Call me crazy, but I just couldn't figure out how he was able to get home from school, be at home for all of 5 minutes and have completed all of his homework. Needless to say, he had lied about doing his homework so that he could play video games; like many of us once were as children, he was an addict. Lol. Now that I think about it, I bet rooming with my younger brother was a complete setup. My parents planned for me to be his "homework checker" all along. lol

I didn't mind checking his homework, or even asking him whether or not he finished his homework. In reality, I wish I had a big brother who would do that for me. Joshua would be annoyed at how I would constantly make him erase incorrect spelling and grammatical errors and get it right, but I assured him, he would be grateful in years to come. I needed for him to get his priorities in order so that he would be prepared for the real world. Outside of our classroom sessions, I let him know that if anyone messes with him, to come and get me. I was his big brother, sworn to protect him as my big brothers once protected me.

I remember back in 1998, I had just graduated from 8th grade and my mom had bought us Seasons Passes to Six Flags Over Georgia. I would go to Six Flags every single day of the summer. And then came the responsibility; my mom said, "Take your brother Joshua with you". Maybe she wanted the house completely vacant so that she could spend time alone with her husband (my step-father) but I'd like to think she primarily wanted my brother and I to spend more quality time together. ☺

My mom was quite clever, you never knew what she was up to, but in some way shape or fashion, she found a way to bring us all together. Breakfast, lunch and dinnertime was the easiest way to bring us together because us boys had huge appetites and were always excited about our next home cooked meal. Church was another way my mom would bring the family together;

we hardly ever missed a Sunday. If all else fails, she would simply say "Go outside and don't come back until XYZ time".

My sister Jordi was the second oldest, and the only girl, so naturally we would protect her. She's smart, pretty, ambitious , has a great heart, and had a close relationship with my mom. Needless to say, I formed an alliance with her early on in my childhood. ☺ What I admired the most about my sister was her ambition, her drive and her ability to create something out of nothing. She would advise me on education, business and relationships, and because she was so successful at all 3, I was pretty much all ears.

I would write letters to my older brothers and send pictures, hoping they would be free soon, and my prayers were soon answered. After years of not having my brothers around, one came back, soon followed by the other. Time apart will allow you to see the value in being together. After so much space and time between us, my older brothers were no longer ashamed to introduce me to their networks, in fact, they wanted to be introduced to mine. And I couldn't be more proud to do so because this is another opportunity I have to bond with my brothers.

I was thrilled to hear from my stepbrother Aaron recently, he told me he needed a suit for a special occasion. I haven't seen him in years, but that didn't matter, I wanted to have a closer relationship with him, so I was more than happy to help. We sat, we ate, and we talked about life, love and relationships for hours. Growing up we didn't see a lot of him, but when he did come around, we were beyond excited to see him because we missed him and our fellowship with him. He was my stepfather's son from a previous marriage, but we loved him simply as our brother.

In college, I met two brothers from another mother, Kerry and Khayri. We called ourselves "Triple Threat", we graduated from Texas Wesleyan University, class of 2008; same class but different fields, we were all athletes, and were very popular on campus. What I admired about these two brothers is they were goal oriented, intelligent, and they were extremely down to earth. We connected right away through our love for music, food, sports and of course the ladies. ☺ We were there for each other no matter what and remain in constant contact long after graduation.

In life, you will come across many men who don't have fathers, brothers or friends to talk to, bond with or network with. It's important to be open and willing to extend yourself as a brother because there are men who are waiting for your fellowship, are missing your fellowship, and desire to have a closer relationship with you. It's ok to be the listening ear, the shoulder to cry on or provide the positive words of advice to another man. That's what being a brother is all about.

Be A Man Of Integrity

It takes a lot to be a good man, that's why being a good man is so admirable amongst other good people. It takes discipline, sacrifice and a long track record of good decision making to bring out these great qualities, and that's what will set you apart. It's easy to take the low road because there's no challenge, no one holding you accountable, and no one pushing you to be better. On the high road, you'll find other people who are constantly making better decisions, reaching for new heights and encouraging one another along the way. The beauty of having integrity is that those who also have it will recognize it inside of you, which will establish trust and prompt the start of a meaningful relationship.

Society is filled with people who lack integrity, which is why we as a people *must* be governed by regulated officials and authorities to ensure that we all live in fairness. Just imagine watching a sports game with no referees… the game would never end because it would boil down to integrity. And when a championship is on the line, you can count on *integrity* going right out of the window. It will be a matter of his word against theirs, so in the end who do we believe? If you choose the team on the left, you'll upset the team on the right and vice versa. To eliminate these problems, we bring in a number of referees who are held to a higher standard and will call the game in fairness.

You don't have to be an elected official to choose to live by a higher standard, you can simply be a son, brother, husband, father or friend. Your peers will respect you more if you have established yourself as someone who has good character and can be trusted. How do you build trust? It's simple, all you have to do is be the best man you can be, and that will require doing the right thing for yourself and for others. Your ability to prove yourself worthy of trust will be the staple that holds your relationship with other people together.

When you apply for a job, they'll ask a series of questions that reflect your work history, educational background, demographic and criminal history. All of the information provided on the application is relevant to the employer because before hiring you, they want to have an idea of who you are. They also want to feel confident in knowing that you are not only capable of doing the job, but also that you can be trusted with their resources and information. By being honest on your application despite how you feel it may hurt or improve your chances, you'll build trust with that employer. They're going to do a background check anyway, and the truth is bound to come out, so give them ahead start by being open and honest from the beginning.

In today's times, people are always on guard because they're so used to other people trying to manipulate or cheat a system to make it work in their favor. By being transparent, having integrity and being honest, you will have great success in not only bringing down those walls, but also in opening up new doors. It's a breath of fresh air to have someone around their friends, family and/or business that can be trusted. If you can manage to be that breathe of fresh air, people will not only *want* to have you around, but they will *need* to have you around. Make yourself indispensable by offering an open and honest relationship that is built on trust.

When establishing your inner circles at school or at work, the first thing people will notice about you is your character. People are interested in knowing who you are as a person, and once they figure you out, the information gathered will be the determining factor in who sticks around and who keeps their distance. Once you show that you have integrity, people will feel more comfortable about opening doors that lead to their wisdom, their network, and their resources. There will be subliminal tests thrown your way such as conversations about your relationships with women, money, time and God. It may seem like *nothing* initially, but to them, your relationship with women, money, time and God is in fact EVERYTHING!

People want to know about your relationship with other women because it reflects what you stand for as a man. People will be particularly interested in you relationship with your mother because she is the woman who brought you into this world. She laid down the foundation and has set the standard by which you will treat the woman you associate with in the future. Sometimes the opportunity to have morals, values and principles instilled in you by your mother is missed, and that has considerable influence on how you interact with other women as a whole. This information is extremely valuable to a man who has a sister, daughter or a wife. A man who knows his role looks to protect the women in his family against all possible threats, even if that means keeping a barrier between him and you.

Women are very sensitive, very delicate and look to a man for protection. For this reason, a woman of substance makes a man wait to get close to her heart and body. She wants to be sure that he can be trusted with it and that he won't intentionally cause her grief and pain. Having a track record of being loyal, respectful, fair and kind will expedite your progress with a woman, as she will have lowered her guards just for *you*. If you want a woman to stay, give her hope. If you want a woman to leave, give her doubt!

People want to know about your relationship with money because it reflects your values and discipline. A man who values money and shows discipline can also be trusted with it and around it. By having a healthy relationship with money, people will feel more comfortable inviting you into their home and around their business and resources. Being a good steward of money will also propel your relationship with others to new heights because they will view you as someone who could help them do the same. The more people see value in you, the more they will want to invest in you.

People want to know about your relationship with time because they don't want theirs to be wasted. If a person doesn't make the best of your time, they shouldn't be blessed with your time. They will look to see what you've done, what you're doing and what your plans are for the future. It's easy to pretend that you're making progress and making moves, but to a person who's *really* doing it, they'll be able to see right through you. Being honest about your progress in life will allow others to see what you are missing from your life as well as what they can add to your life. Your time is too valuable to waste it on people who aren't going places, and other people will feel the same way about you.

How you spend your time and whom you spend your time with is important in the realm of building relationships. Take public figures for example, they cannot afford to be seen associating with people who lack integrity because that makes them guilty by association. The association with someone who makes poor decisions with their time is also a reflection of them and can hinder their progress in life. By spending your time doing positive things, you'll attractive more positive people and opportunities. If you're having trouble figuring out how to stay positive, simply surround yourself with positive people.

People want to know about your relationship with God because your level of spirituality portrays that you acknowledge a power that is greater than you. Submission to this higher power keeps you humble, influences your attitude towards others. Not only will your relationship with God help your relationship with others, but it will help you to build a relationship with yourself. You will begin to see the value in you, understand your worth, and use your findings to inspire others. God is love, and when you make a spiritual connection, you will start doing things out of love.

Your reputation is everything, so protect it at all costs. It's easier to walk in truth than to fight over a lie. Every day you should look to improve as a man, and you do this by being proactive and always aspiring to have more. There's no such thing as a free lunch, so take pride in working your way up to the top, and when you get there, help others get there too. Life is about building relationships and leaving behind legacies, so start building yours today. When you leave this earth, stories will be told about the way you lived your life and the things you achieved. You are in a position to write your own story in the way you want others to tell it, and that's by living in truth.

When others speak about your character, you want them to speak highly of you and to want to model after you. You want people to be inspired by your struggle, inspired by your failures and inspired by your success.

Be Confident

In effective leadership, you have to appear to be sure about yourself and your decisions even if you're not. In order for others to respect your leadership, they first have to believe that you are bold enough to speak up, speak out and fight for what you believe in. Most people are still searching for this air of confidence in themselves, so when they see it in you, you will give them something to model after. The sole purpose of leadership is to inspire others to achieve their goals; to be better, do better and have better. Before anyone else will believe in your mission and follow suit, you first must prove that you believe in yourself.

I decided to take up photography when I was a sophomore in college. I had no professional training, nor did I have all of the professional equipment that a pro might have. All I knew was that I wanted to creatively capture people's images. At first people were skeptical because out of nowhere I made a transition in my life and decided I wanted to photograph people. Capturing someone's likeness or image is a very intimate moment and can make some people feel uncomfortable. It didn't help that I was known for being the comic and wasn't to be taken seriously at all.

I would continue to work at my craft despite my ignorance in the field, and other people's doubts. I even had a to borrow a friend of mine's point and shoot digital camera to get started. Over time, my lighting improved, my exposure was correct and my composition was spot on. I would take pictures of any cheerleaders, athletes and friends who would allow me to. I didn't do it for the money, I did it for the passion; I simply loved photography.

It was right around the time when Facebook started to take off; I had access to friends from many different colleges in Texas. After posting samples of my work, my portfolio was grabbing the attention of students from all over and I was soon offered a photography position at our school newspaper "The Rambler". Today, my work has been featured in major magazines, newspapers, books and other publications. The same people who wouldn't allow me to take their pictures for free then, would pay me now. Had I not believed in myself, I would've quit at the first sign of rejection, which would have hindered me from my own success.

Often times, people will discourage you not because they don't believe in *you*, but because they don't believe in themselves. They don't have what it takes to uplift you high enough; they fear that once you reach your goals, you will leave them behind. It's up to you to be confident enough in yourself and your abilities, and open up the doors to your future. Doing so will inspire everyone who remembers where you came from and how much you've accomplished. In addition, it will inspire those who are in a position to help you get to the next level to work with you, as they will see value in your ambition and drive.

Confidence is so attractive because not everyone has it! When you don't portray it, people will begin to doubt you. When you do portray it, people will begin believe in you. If you can manage to get others to subscribe to your thoughts, your ideals and your vision, then you will have attained *true* power! Without confidence, you will have a hard time getting others to subscribe much of anything you do.

Confidence helps build trust, as people will grow to rely on your leadership. Once that trust is broken, you will notice a decrease in moral. The thing they admired the most about you has been lost, leaving an ambiguous sense of direction. People who are looking for hope won't feel comfortable being led by a man who isn't sure about his next move(s). To avoid this, you have to be honest with yourself and figure out a plan for your life before including others.

Being confident in yourself or the lack thereof will tremendously impact your relationship with women. I know because I've lived it. After much soul searching I've been able to identify with my strengths and my weaknesses. This process has helped me to use my strengths to gather people who could benefit from them, and could also help me overcome my weaknesses. Not only did I have confidence in myself, but also because of who *they* were, we attracted one another and I had confidence in them.

It took years for me to gain confidence with the opposite sex; I was the second youngest of 5 boys and 1 girl and they seemed to be *naturals*. It would amaze me how my brothers were able to walk right up to a woman, introduce themselves and then walk away either with *her*, her number or both! This was something I had never done before and I would often hide how much I liked a girl simply because I didn't know how to approach her. I was more likely to write her a love note and sent it through a friend than to walk up to her and initiate conversation. I was afraid of being rejected by a girl, but more importantly, I had not developed the confidence in myself.

Anytime I would hang out with my brothers or go places with my parents, women would say "Cheyenne is the cutest one" "Cheyenne is going to be a heartbreaker when he gets older" and all I could think when I was a child was "Pffffft yea right. I can't even muster up the confidence to talk to a girl." I was young, interested in getting to know a girl or two, but the problem for me was, I had not yet gotten to know myself. I didn't take the time to give myself credit for all the great qualities I had and the qualities I portrayed on a daily basis. I had not taken into account that I had value, I had worth and that I would be a great asset to someone else's life.

For years, I would pretend that I had lost my virginity so that my older brothers and male friends wouldn't make fun of me. Sex? Pffffft, I was a sophomore in high school when I got my first French kiss. I was shaking in my boots thinking, "Please don't let her try to make a move on me". The girls have always been attracted to me back when I was in school, I simply didn't know how to handle the attraction. And for some reason, even in my teens, the girls I would attract would always be far more advanced than I was.

In a way, I suppose my slowness to get them in bed tremendously raised my value. I was very much sexually attracted to them, I simply did not have the experience, and wasn't ready to put my reputation on the line in the event that I "came up short". I was very popular at school, as I tended to focus more on personality and character than anything else. I was well known for entertaining and making people laugh, and that was an area that I felt truly confident in. The more my popularity grew, the more the girls grew to like me and wanted to get close to me.

To make matters worse, my family moved around a lot throughout my childhood, so I would constantly have to make new friends all over again. From Pre-K to 12th grade, I've attended a grand total of 10 different schools. I was always the "new kid", having to constantly prove myself, fit in and stay relevant. This was a great experience for me as I had the opportunity to go to new places, meet new people and experiences new things that I wouldn't have had I stayed in one spot. I was being prepared for the real world; figuring out how to adapt to any and every environment.

Then their was Homecoming, and then prom, both of which is was customary to invite a date. I knew exactly whom I wanted to bring to both of those dances however she was coincidentally taken. Her mate was older, had more experience, had an edge and was the total opposite of me. I on the other hand was the good guy who didn't take any risks, played things safe and didn't offer any type of adventure. That's when I had my epiphany; I then understood that a woman of substance wants to be led by a man who dares to be bold, dares to be different and dares to be great!

Whenever you come up with an idea and speak things into existence, there will be supporters and there will be doubters. What people will admire the most is the faith you have in your words, your strengths and your abilities. Once spoken, people will keep a close eye on you to see how far you're willing to go to make it come into fruition. This is why some women are so turned on by men who never stopped pursuing them after years of being turned down. Even after countless rejections, you are fearless in your approach, totally sure of yourself and hopefully that she will have a change of heart. What they see is a man that truly believes that if he stays focused and never gives up, he will one day achieve his goal.

This paradigm shift made me look at myself in a whole new light! I had everything I needed to attract a woman all along, I simply needed to love it, nurture it and when it was the right season, watch it bloom. There was nothing that I needed to do that anyone else was doing, I simply had to show a woman *my* worth and give her a reason to choose *me*. That's where the saying "There's something about you" comes from; people identify with a person who has successfully tapped into their true power and are capable of projecting energy that is desired by others. Confidence is attractive!

Respect Yourself

If you don't respect yourself, you'll take away other people's motivation to respect you too. No matter what societies standards are, you must create a standard of your own that best represents you. After all, it's your name and your legacy that's on the line and not societies. When people say your name, you want a certain image to be ingrained in their minds that present you only in a positive light. Your name and your reputation is everything, so you must protect it and preserve it at all cost.

My name Cheyenne Bostock represents everything I stand for and everything I am. Anytime my name is placed in headlines, it serves as a way to inform others of my association with that particular organization. For this reason, I must be conscious of the way I carry myself and treat others, for bad news spreads far faster than good. It's important to have a good standing relationship with the people in your community, church, schools and the media because these are the people who will echo your name for whatever reasons that suit them. Word of mouth is the most powerful form of marketing so let your actions influence the things other people say. These echoes will reach people who may know you, but also people who have never met you.

Making a good name for yourself isn't solely about appearances, it's primarily about integrity and good character. Do the right thing, so people can always use that against you. There will come a time in every person's life where we won't have the opportunity to speak for ourselves, and you will want your prior actions to have done all of the talking for you. The proof will always be in your actions, and there isn't enough deception in the world to cover up your lack of kindness and servitude here on earth.

When I first started coaching other people's relationships, I had to make a judgment call. I could either use my relationship insight and years of studying behavioral patterns to create a cult of manipulators, or I could use it to create an army of influencers. I knew that spewing out manipulative relationship advice would be seen as valuable to manipulators, but it would hold no value to those who were looking to learn and grow. Consequently, my credibility as a relationship expert would be null and void if I merely focused on how a man could solely win over a woman or vice versa. A relationship is about creating a win/win situation for both parties involved, which is better known as *compromise*.

I had to choose long-term victory over short-term, which has not only improved my career as a Life & Relationship Expert, but also as a man. You will be faced with this same dilemma many times over, and will have to choose right from wrong. No one is perfect and we all make mistakes, but what's important is that you learn from them. Learning from your mistakes will show that you have grown as a man, and people will respect you more for it. In fact, if you haven't made mistakes in your life, you're either in denial, or not normal.

Back when I was a kid in school, I would make plenty of mistakes and still do today. In fact, I don't even know if you could even call them mistakes; I was simply young, dumb and was making poor decisions. The most important observation that I could make was that I had not yet learned my lesson. This was a problem for me because since I hadn't learned my lesson, I was apt to make the same mistakes again. This could land me in big trouble if the consequences or my actions turned out to be too severe the next time around.

When you're in school and other social clubs, one thing all men experience is a close association with other men, and we hope that in time we will gain a closer association with other women. You'll hear stories about how many women they've slept with, who they've slept with, when and where, and you'll feel pressured into believing that this is what it means to be a man. On the contrary, degrading and disgracing women is not what it means to be a man; this type of behavior shows that *he* has not yet grown into a man. He doesn't respect women as the gift from God that they are, which also reveals that he doesn't respect himself. When a man respects himself, he carries himself with honor, dignity and respect and closely associates with others who do the same.

It's true that you are the company that you keep. Show me your best friend and I will show you the type of man you are. Even if you're not guilty, you'll be guilty by association. Choosing the company you keep is a reflection of whom you are inside, as it is *you* who is making the conscious decision to associate. Once you are old enough to make decisions, you will be held accountable, and people will respect your either more or less based on your affiliation with others.

Every decision you make today effects tomorrow. Most people want their past to be erased because they're ashamed of it and don't want it to come up in the future. Your past is and always will be relevant to your future, which is why it's so important to respect yourself and others today. Consider what your actions would do to your name, or what it would mean for your son or daughter to have to also bear your name in years to come. Consider your parents and their legacy and how it would shame them to be associated with anything disgraceful. Most figure they don't have to be responsible and accountable until they turn 18.

When you're 18, no one excuses your behavior like they normally would a child, and you conveniently want others to respect you as an adult. You want the right to vote, pump gas and smoke cigarettes, but don't want to be charged as an adult in a crime. You want to be able to come and go as you please in your parents' house, but you don't want to pay rent. You want to have unprotected sex, but have no means of provided for an unexpected child. In actuality, you will find yourself demanding respect because you haven't grown enough us a man to command it.

Through actions, you can prove that you deserve respect and you can start by respecting yourself. You can show your respect for self by treating yourself with dignity and respect and valuing people, time, money and resources. You can show your respect for people by acknowledging their skills, being supportive and sharing your time and resources. You can show your respect for time by keeping a schedule, being on time and requiring that others do the same. You can show your respect for money by being financially responsible, budgeting your money and being charitable to others.

Treat everyone with dignity and respect not because of who *they* are, but because of who *you* are. Your respect for others isn't always about what you say; it's also about what you do. Ultimately it boils down to how much respect you have for yourself as an individual. The way you walk, talk, dress and carry yourself will influence the type of people you attract. When I was in high school, I was on the Men's Varsity basketball team under coach Bob Hurley and I had heard that we weren't allowed to have braids, tattoos or girlfriends.

At the time, I was growing my hair out, and I actually had just taken out my twists before transferring to the school. I was the fairly new kid, and one day, after a frustrating practice, coach finished a statement by saying "Oh yea, and Cheyenne, cut your hair!" The whole team looked at me and were holding in their laughter because they knew how much I wanted to grow my hair. I knew that if I came back to practice without a haircut, he would take it as I didn't respect him, and if I showed up at a game without a haircut, I for sure wouldn't get to play. The girls liked the "Kobe Bryant" look I had going on and I was torn.

Needless to say, I cut my hair, returned to school and practice and showed my coach that I did respect him and wanted his mutual respect. It's important to have a respectful relationship amongst people who are in positions of authority, especially if it in some way can help or harm your future. You'll increase your chances of gaining their respect if you carry yourself as someone who commands it. Yielding to authority is a sign of humility and grace, and will make people who are in authority *feel* superior even if they aren't. That's the thing about respect, it's not an admission of an individual's power or the lack thereof, and it's simply an acknowledgment of their position.

As it pertains to self-respect, you must realize that what you're working towards is *positioning* yourself for future acknowledgment. When people see your face and hear your name, you want to be acknowledged for the work you've been doing. That brings forth the question of whether or not you are in fact worthy of being acknowledged. What have you been doing with your life? Do you spend your time serving yourself or serving others? Do you focusing on hurting people or helping people? You don't have to answer; the proof will be evident in everything around you.

Respect Women

Its amazing how *strong* women are; no matter what the world throws at them, they somehow find the strength and the resources to overcome it. They raise us to become great men, they give birth to our children, and they keep our houses in order and run our businesses. Words can't even describe how *awesome* women are and how much they make this world a better place. If not for a woman, we would not even be here! Our women play such a huge role in the makeup of a man, and for that reason we must forever honor them.

When I look back at my childhood I often wonder how my mother did it. She raised 5 boys and 1 girl, not to mention catering to her husband. For me, raising one child was tough, and she raised 6! That was impressive (to me); we always had a roof over our head, great birthday's and Christmas, back to school clothes, Easter outfits, you name it. There were even times where we were all in private schools. She made sure we had everything we needed and then some, and it is greatly appreciated.

Often times, we don't give women enough credit for their brilliance and their strength, and that in itself poses a problem. Everyone wants to feel valued and appreciated, and this requirement isn't gender specific. It's important for us as men to remember who were are and what we mean to a woman. Women look to us for leadership, they value our opinion, and they want to be acknowledged and respected by us. Our validation helps to keep them motivated to continue being great mothers, wives, sisters, friends and influential women of society.

It bothers me terribly when I hear a man call a woman out of her name, and even worse when it's someone who is significant to them such as the mother of their child or worse, their own mother. Growing up in a house with a bunch of brothers, we were almost always rough with one another; rarely were we kind to each other. It was like a non-stop competition of who was the fastest, smartest, or best looking. We did however treat our sister with more dignity and respect simply because she was a woman.

For as long as I can remember, the lesson for men was to forever honor his mother, always be a gentlemen and never hit a female. These were the standard rules that applied to any and every man, and for some reason women deemed it necessary to vocalize. Maybe they've experienced a son who didn't respect them and their relationship has fallen apart because of it. Maybe their husband failed at being a gentleman and the marriage didn't last. Maybe they were once in an abusive relationship and are still suffering from it.

Or maybe they just want to make certain that you turn out to be the best man you can be. After all, women are best known for their strong ability to love and care for others. I appreciate the fact that women are giving men tips on how to cater to a woman, even long before we know what to do with one. Where are the men? Why aren't the men giving these lessons?

The answer is simple; too many men aren't selfless enough to extend this knowledge to other men who are in need. Most men aren't concerned with how other men treat women unless it directly affects them. Growing up, I paid close attention to how women like to be treated and how they should be treated. I didn't have to go far, I simply observed my parents marriage. I observed the way my stepfather would speak to my mother, treat my mother, and carry himself around her.

When he drove us places, he would open up the car door for my mother when we departed and when we arrived. He complimented my mother on her cooking, her cleaning, her home designing and her fantastic job as a mother. Their birthday was one day apart from one another and he would make sure that *her* special day was acknowledged. When he introduced people to her, he introduced her as his wife, then by her name. He showed her through his actions that he respected her for who she was to him.

He had to; otherwise he would have 5 boys after him. There's no way we were going to sit there and watch a man disrespect our mother. No way, no how! If you want to be a part of our mother's life, you had better come correct. She had enough to bear on her shoulders being widowed with 5 children than to have to deal with yet another burden.

You will see the value in knowing how to respect women when it's *your* woman that's on the line. Yes, your pride and joy, your angel, your reason for breathing. Not everyone will see your special lady in that same light. You wouldn't feel too secure about another man touching your woman to get her attention, calling her out of her name, or trying to get her into bed behind your back. Of course you wouldn't because she's *your* lady and hopefully that's not how you treat other women.

You want men to respect your lady not only because she's *your* woman, but simply because she's *a* woman. She deserves to be treated with dignity and respect just like any other person. We don't have the right to grab a woman by the arm and demand that she comes and speaks to us. Nor do we have the right to talk down on her if/when a woman rejects us. And if she says she's taken, you should respect it just as you would want the next man to do the same for your relationship.

Women are not sexual objects, and their purpose here on earth isn't solely to cater to the needs of men. You will have a much better relationship with women when you come to terms that not every woman will be romantically interested in you. Women have to work to make a living just like men, they have to seek education just like men, and they have to build relationships in order to get ahead just like men. Not every conversation or interaction with a woman is an invitation for you to proposition a woman for personal interests. Some women simply want to have a professional and/or platonic relationship.

You're not obligated to agree to those terms, however you must respect a woman's wishes. We all reserve the right to be selective, and sometimes the person she selects won't be you. Out of everything else in the world, a woman wants your respect. We all make choices in our lives, even ones that we regret, but we still should learn to respect one another. No matter who a woman is, or what she's done in her past, when you come into her life, you should either love her or leave her alone.

Every woman has esteem issues, and tries to find a way to cope with them. Often times it results in her degrading herself, and getting a boost of esteem from men. This behavior ranges from women who are prostitutes, strippers, and porn stars, to serial daters, girlfriends and wives. The one thing that all of these women have in common is, they all want to be loved. Somewhere throughout the course of their lives they've lost respect for themselves and they're searching hard to find a way to love themselves again. Throughout that same course, a man (most likely their father) missed the opportunity to love and respect their daughter and show her to do the same for herself.

One of the main reason's society protects women is because they are able to reproduce, and what they reproduce affects the economy. This world needs strong women, women who know they are worthy, know they are valuable, and know that we love them. We have the tools, now we need to start building. We need to start building ourselves up to be better men, start raising better men, and start encouraging our men to protect our women. We need to be better fathers to our daughters, husbands to our wives, and brothers to our sisters.

If we are the leaders, we need to start acting like it and lead only by example. Lets encourage our women to never give up on us, because we will never give up on them. Our women need to see it in our actions and hear it in our words that we value them. Every day should be sister, daughter, mother, and women's day because they never take days off from caring about us men. We need to treat our women as if they are everything, because without them we would be nothing.

Chapter 2:

The Learning Curve

Learn How To Be Responsible

The first thing that comes to mind when I think about what it means to be a man is responsibility. We have a responsibility as men to be leaders, role models, mentors, teachers, advisors and world changers. Anytime I see men doing anything less, I simply think to myself that they haven't yet tapped into their true power and haven't yet found their purpose. When you serve a purpose greater than yourself, you'll become stronger, richer, and wiser because that's what it takes to lead. It builds your character in a way that would prove to be impossible if/when you have no one and nothing holding you accountable.

My son Ethan is a blessing to me because he's someone who holds me accountable no matter what. He doesn't know what rent is, what bills are, or what it means to be in debt. All he knows is that he's a child, I'm his father and he wants the world. I remember one time Ethan wanted to buy something and I told him that I didn't have any cash on me. His reply was, "You know what Daddy? I think we should go to the ATM". I couldn't help but laugh because he really does think money grows on trees. Lol

I love his innocent and I try my best to protect it by not informing of the harsh realities of the world just yet. I say things like "We'll see…" or "If you're a good boy…" or "We have to save in order to get that…" I don't let him know "Son, I just paid the rent, phone bill, went grocery shopping, and bought you new clothes so I can't afford anything else right now". No, I simply let him know what we have to do in order to have the things that we want in the future. I'm a believer that you can have anything you want in life if you plan and work hard to get it.

I don't want to put any doubt in my sons mind about my ability or his ability to achieve his goals because fear and doubt is hazardous to your success. Instead I enforce the notion of valuing a dollar and not buying on impulse simply because it's there. I do this by encouraging my son to use his own money to buy the things that he wants. Thankfully, this hasn't backfired on me; I'm aware that with $5, Ethan can buy 20 gumballs for 25 cents and say "What Daddy? I used my own money". Lol I show him how to manage the money that he's been given by not spending it all at once.

Money management is only one of my many responsibilities as a man and as a father. I use my son as an example because who knows what my life would be like without him. I spend my weekends doing activities with my son, and those moments are priceless. If he weren't in the picture there's no telling what my weekends would consist of. Now that I have a son, I think about my future, our future, I plan ahead because now I'm responsible not only for myself, but also for him.

There's tuition for school, medical, food, clothes, birthdays, Christmas and many other miscellaneous expenses associated with having a child and it's all worth it. It gives me a reason to wake up and work hard every day so that I can rest knowing he's taken care of.

It gives me great pleasure knowing that my son can sleep worry free at night with a roof over his head and food on his table. It's hard enough being a kid, learning the ways of the world, and fitting in with society, the last thing I need is my son worrying about the stability of his home. And it gives your child a sense of pride knowing that their father is out there working hard, being responsible and taking care of his business.

Stepping out on faith and crossing over into a new venture sometimes can be scary, but it's time to overcome your fears. I know countless men who are living with women not because they love her and are interested in building a future with her, but because the rent is free. They're too afraid to go out, get a job, save up money and invest in a home of their own. The woman is their security net and they've fallen back on it with no plans of ever leaving. Not only is this unfair to the woman, but it's crippling to them as a man.

Being responsible means that you are *taking* responsibility, not just being given it. You are voluntarily going out and applying for a jobs each and everyday until you get one. You are spending less and saving more so that you can afford your own apartment. You are buying more groceries and cooking instead of eating out because it saves you money that you can't afford to spend. You are actively looking for an apartment so that you can move out on your own.

Being responsible requires you to make changes in your life that will impact your life and the lives of those around you. That means you have to be on time, you have to return things that you've borrowed, you have pay back your debts, and you have to follow through with the promises you've made. Your word needs to count for something, and your actions need to count for more. When you are responsible, people will see it, and will trust you with their time and valued possessions as a result. When you prove to be irresponsible, you will burn bridges that you need to walk over in order to build relationships and be successful.

I've learned over time to say yes to the right people and say no to the wrong people. To me it doesn't matter how long we've known each other, whether or not we're related by blood, etc. If you have a track record of being irresponsible, then I'm not going to trust you with things that are of value to me. You have to work to build that trust, and until you do, the answer to your request will be no. I'd much rather *give* a family member $20 than to sit there and listen to them ask to *borrow* $20. We both know that you can't be trusted, are terrible with money, and have absolutely no way of getting the money back.

But when you've proven that you are someone who is considerate of others, good with money and trustworthy, getting a loan is no problem at all. You see, the power of being responsible goes far beyond your own personal benefit. It trickles down to relationship with other people, other businesses and other brands. People want to know that you value your own time and money and that you manage it well. Then and only then will they be willing to sacrifice their own. This is something that you will experience when you apply for a job, a house or a car.

People who are irresponsible, manage money poorly, and aren't good with time management often complain about *standards*. How could they possibly understand standards? All their lives they've skated by, cut corners and cheated the system. Those people are in for a rude awakening and for them I say, "Welcome to the real world". A world where there are background checks, credit checks and oh yes we need references. We want to know who in their right mind will vouch for your mess.

Standards are something that's extremely important to me, and when I'm dating I go through a series of questions that reveal a woman's character and position in life. I want to know their age, educational background, career, number of children, marital status, current living situation, and what went wrong in their last relationship. The answer to these questions will give me all the information I need as to whether or not I feel a woman is deserving of my time. No matter how beautiful a woman may be, it's important to me that she has substance and depth to her.

I need to know that she is educated, career oriented, financial secure, emotionally available and prepared to grow in a relationship. If she's not then there's no sense in me dating her because if she's not taking good care of herself, how could she take good care of me? Women look at men the same way; they want to know that you are capable of taking care of yourself and your responsibilities. If you can't take care of your own responsibilities, how could you take care of her? The same applies to a successful company going through a hiring process.

How can they trust a man who is always late, never pays his bills, has no major accomplishments in his life, and no goals with a Fortune 500 company? That's not to say that you won't get lucky and find a woman or a job who will take a chance on you, but your chances will be greater when you take responsibility for your actions. If you are an able bodied man, you can do anything you put your mind to, and that's exactly what *people* want to see. They want to see you be a great father, great husband, great worker, great leader so that they can feel more comfortable about including you in their lives. They want to see you achieve your goals and serve as motivation to help them reach theirs.

You'll feel so much better about yourself when you've taken those first few steps and overcome your fears. Feel good knowing that you've worked hard for the job you have, the house you bought, the children you've raised, or the wife you've pleased. As a man you are expected to set goals, break barriers, and lead others into prosperity, but you first need to know how to get there yourself. Take pride in holding yourself accountable for your obligation to this world. Don't be afraid to take action, be prepared to take action.

Learn How To Manage Money

Two things that men value the most in life are our time and our money. Our time gives us the opportunity to build relationships, find happiness and make a difference in this world. Our money helps us to further reach those goals. In order to be successful at building relationships, finding happiness and making a difference in the world, we must learn to properly manage one of the things that help us to do so. Our money has the power that we give it, but before we give it, we must place some sort of value on it.

When I was a kid, I placed high value on pennies, but apparently not *everyone* did. I would find pennies inside of the couch, outside on the ground, on the floors of stores, you name it. Since nobody else wanted them, I would pick them up, put them in my piggy bank and over time would wrap them up in 50-cent wrappers and eventually spend them. I remember asking my family members to save their pennies just for me. They happily obliged and every time I saw them, I had a few dollars that I could spend (in pennies). These brown, dirty coins meant the world to me because it afforded me everything that I wanted at the time.

My appreciation for pennies as a child has helped me tremendously as an adult because I learned how to appreciate money right down to the cent. I also realized that if I wanted to have more than just pennies, I wouldn't find them lying around on the ground, in my couch or on the floor of a grocery store, but I had to earn it. My mother had 5 boys and 1 girl, so if you can imagine, money had to stretch over all of us, and if we wanted anything extra, we had to earn it. My siblings and I caught on to this early on and began our entrepreneurial endeavors. We knew that no matter how much money we earned while we were out hustling, we had to make it stretch over time.

I would always wonder where my older brothers were getting their extra money from, because I knew for sure that my mom wouldn't dare overlook *me* (the obedient one) lol and give only to my brothers. They finally let me in on their secret and told me they were bagging groceries at Shop Rite at Route 440 in Jersey City. I was excited because this was something that I could do; all I had to do was get my older brothers to take me with them. They soon obliged and I immediately went to work bagging groceries, pushing their carts to their cars and getting tipped for my good service.

I had more money in my pocket than ever (tax free), not that I knew what taxes were at 9 years old. Now what to do with all this money? Hmmmm! I bought popcorn, pretzels, a hero, oodles of noodles, a case of soda, fruit snacks, and kept the rest for a rainy day. I was in HEAVEN! The best part was we all had our own money, so we didn't have to try our usual scheme to mooch off of one another's "dough". This was my first taste of financial independence; money that I earned on my own that didn't come from my mom.

As the money came and went, I quickly learned what it meant to *earn* a living and be financially responsible. I enjoyed when the money came, and was sad when the money went. I had to figure out how to get the money to stay in my account otherwise I'll never truly be financially free. I know, these aren't the typical worries of a 9 year old, but my entrepreneurial spirit kicked in early! I wanted what I wanted when I wanted it and I didn't want to have to depend on my mother to give it to me.

For a lot of young men, there are no lessons on what to do with a dollar once he gets it. This often results in a boy who grows into a man not understanding the value of money. When there's no value in principle placed on a dollar, he'll treat it as if it's *just* a dollar. But no, it's more than just $1, it's a tool that can help you build anything you want in life, all you need is a blueprint. When you think about an infrastructure, there's a blueprint for what someone foresee coming to life in the future. There's also an advisory board consisting of stakeholders, contractors, and investors who are involved in the process of the development.

Before the shovel even hits the dirt, there is a plan on what to do with every dollar invested; also known as a *budget*. This budget is designed to invest in anything that will add value to the overall progress and help avoid any overspending. This way when you decide to go into your bank account to make withdrawals, you have a certain amount allocated to whatever it is you're doing while leaving some left over. Without a budget, you'll be prone to empty out the entire account and spend with no end in sight. This is fast and easy way to stay broke, by not budgeting your money.

Figure out what your expenses are on a daily, weekly, monthly and yearly basis and try to keep them at a minimum. If you can avoid adding on new expenses, by all means do so. Your fixed expenses such as your rent, car note, cell phone bill, transportation, food, etc should be accounted for in advance. If your expenses outweigh your income, you'll either have to cut down your expenses or figure out a way to generate more income. Maybe a cheaper rates plan on your cell phone, or cut down on driving and take public transportation. The idea is to balance out your account to where you have more coming in than going out.

This will help you gain the financial freedom that you desire which will give you more time to spend with your family friends and loved ones. With all of these things, you will gain peace of mind. Managing your money isn't something that's impossible; it's simply something that you have to work towards. You have to learn to respect the money that you earn, and use it to invest in things that will yield a return. The more you invest in things that yield a return, the more returns you'll have coming in. If you spend every dollar that you have, you'll have to work longer and harder to keep money coming in.

If you're working a full-time and you're always broke, it's not the *income* that's the problem it's the *outcome*. The money is there, but the person who possesses it isn't making the best use of it. Anytime you get a dollar in your hand you should think to yourself, "How can I turn this $1 into more?". If you have that kind of attitude towards money, you'll find yourself on the receiving end of more it. Work smarter, not harder.

When I was six years old, I was hit by a car and the judge awarded me a large settlement that I would receive once I turned 21. When I was six, I would say I would use the money to buy my mom a house, and would disregard any siblings who were ever mean to me. Lol As I grew older, and as my feelings towards my mother changed (typical kid) and as my financial responsibilities grew, my mind slowly changed in regards to what I thought I would do with the money. I was a sophomore in college and boy could I use the money. I took a lump sum as opposed to receiving payments every 5 years.

I thought to myself "Tomorrow's not promised, and if I'm smart about my investment, I'll have made far more money than this settlement could offer by the time I'm able to receive it". I invested in a new laptop, made a payment on my school tuition, put some in the bank, and invested $10,000 into my new photography equipment. To date, I've made that money many times over with my photography business and am very much satisfied with the decision I've made to pursue my passion. I could've went on a crazy shopping spree with the money, but that would not yield me any future return. The goal for me was to invest in something that could forever generate income.

When you make your first investment, and it goes well, share it with your close family members and friends. This is a great way to build relationships with them and to show them where you are in life. When people see that you are buying your first home, starting your own business, or giving to charity, you'll motivate them to want to do the same. People want to be surrounded by positive and successful people, so make sure that you make the cut. The way to get invited into these circles is to simply focus on your life, your business and your finances and work towards success.

All it takes is discipline, a set of goals and a plan of action and you are on your way to becoming the financially responsible adult you are destined to be. This will help boost your esteem, improve your level of confidence, increase your chances of a successful relationship with a woman, and expand your network. When your money is right, you'll have more room to have fun and enjoy life, which you'll more than likely want to do now that you can afford it. You'll go out more, meet new people and experience new things, and that's what life is all about. Before you can distribute the money, you first have to learn how to handle the money.

Figure out your strong points, your passion, and your desire, then work in a field that will help you grow spiritually as well as financially. Pay your tithes, pay yourself, and *then* take care of your other expenses. Have a set amount of money that you keep in savings each month and avoid the temptation to spend it. Invest in others not only in money but also with your time and you will open up doors that yield great financial and spiritual returns. Have a budget set aside for emergencies, charitable giving and personal leisure. With all the money and blessings that come your way, don't forget to give back and create opportunities for generations to come.

Learn How To Listen

One of the greatest gifts in the world is the ability to listen and observe. So much value information can be gathered simply by being quiet and still. You will find that when engaging others, people will sometimes reveal so many things about their personality and character through your silence. In fact, through your silence, you will open up the door for others to walk right in and enlighten you. Through listening, you will gain new perspective, insight and ideals that would not have otherwise come.

I love talking to my 7-year-old son, but what I love even more is listening to him. When I listen, my son shares so many of his innermost thoughts and feelings to me. His mind is always full of ideas and creativity and I want him to feel comfortable making those ideas a reality. A lot of parents are quick to tell their child to "Shut Up" or "Stop Talking", but I want him to do the opposite. If my son loves to talk, then I will learn how to love to listen. Perhaps his love for talking could lead to future speaking opportunities as an actor, journalist or maybe a politician.

Either way, I want my son to get in the habit of finding a positive outlet to creatively express himself. As his father, it's my job to help groom him and help him perfect whatever craft he decides to take on. Through observation, I've learned that my son likes to read, write, draw, act, dance, run and do gymnastics. Not only does he enjoy doing it, he's actually great at it. By listening to his dreams and encouraging him, I establish myself as a go-to source for him to express himself.

One day I received a phone call from my son's mother telling me that his teacher has requested a parent-teacher conference. When I inquired as to what the meeting was about, she said that our son Ethan had been misbehaving more than usual and that it needed to be addressed. In my mind, I thought that this would be a great opportunity to talk with my son, and ask questions regarding what was going on. I was preparing my heart and mind to listen and get information as opposed to striking fear into his heart.

His mother went on to tell me that she had taken disciplinary actions *literally* into her own hands. As a man who was once physically disciplined by a woman (my mother), I know for certain that that is no way to get a young boy to open up. After expressing to her what my experience was like with my mother as a child, we agreed that that type of disciplinary action would no longer take place and that we will use more positive ways to discipline our son. I had a flash back at that moment and I remembered how I would much rather have had a heart to heart conversation over a belt any day. By the time I got the chance to speak to my son, I knew he had already had enough, and I knew he would be in no mood to talk, let alone give me access to his feelings.

I would wait until the weekend when the smoke was clear and he's in a better mood, having totally forgotten about the recent occurrences at school. Not only was I preparing myself to remain calm and come up with the right words to say, I was also preparing myself for what I might hear. I didn't want the answer that I would get during the moment when it was happening. That answer would only be enough to protect him from what was yet to come. I wanted the answer that was honest and true, and my strategy for doing so was to talk to him about it on *his* turf, but on *my* terms.

I would create a safe, loving environment and make him feel comfortable before I would ask him a few questions about his life at school. That's the thing about raising children, they *do* have a life whether we parents want to admit it or not. I have no clue what goes on while my son is at school, but I still need to be in the know. To avoid my son closing himself off to me, I do my best to make him feel comfortable about telling the truth, while still enforcing disciplinary actions. It's important for him to know that I'm here for him, to listen, to learn, and to encourage, however I am still his father and he will be held accountable for his actions.

What's great about listening to your child is that they actually want to be open and honest with you, in most cases, they're simply afraid of what might happen if/when they do. The time where they could make a mistake and be held by you went away when their diapers did. Or worst, the yelling, scolding and the beating is all they know, even from their diaper stages. Now the trust is broken, they don't want to hurt you, and they don't want you to hurt them. So now they've closed you off from the information that could bring you closer together and possibly even save their lives.

Paying attention to details means taking special care of the things that matter to you in life. If you take the time to open up your heart, mind, eyes and ears, your listening will become that much more effective which will enhance the quality of your relationship. It's easy to be present and hear what's going on, but through listening you gain access to the heart of the matter. Getting the information you need through your listening skills will save you a great deal of time, energy, effort and money. It can cost you more than you bargained for if you're not *paying* attention.

Listening has to be pre-meditated in order for you to grasp the heart of the message. You have to be ready and willing to receive the information, otherwise you might miss it. Have you ever overheard something someone else was saying that was either strange, unethical, or funny, but you needed to hear it again because you weren't actually listening? That's because your mind wasn't fixed on registering the information you were about to receive. You weren't prepared for it, therefore you had to spend more time having the message repeated, which more than likely would be watered down the second time you heard it.

When a person has to repeat him or herself, it makes them feel as though you simply weren't listening. In their mind, they're thinking, "I've just said it! Why should I repeat myself to someone who wasn't listening in the first place". Initially, they were enthusiastic about sharing the information because they felt they were sharing it with someone who actually cared. After discovering that you weren't *really* paying attention, it feels as though they were wasting their breath and their time. The last thing you want is for someone you care about to stop informing you on the details that make a difference in their lives.

This theory has the same effect in the workplace. When your boss gives you instructions, clearly it's because there are tasks that need to be delegated to you. If he had the time to do it himself, he probably wouldn't be wasting his value time briefing you. To ensure that he feels you can be trusted with the tasks, be prepared whenever he calls you into his office or whenever he pops into yours. Stop whatever it is you are doing, open your heart, mind, eyes and ears and get ready to receive the information. He will respect the fact that you are giving him your undivided attention, and that you have a pen and pad ready, but also that you have a great attitude about listening to others.

I have a saying that goes "If you're smarter than your boss, act dumber.". I recall working for an employer years ago as an independent contractor, and I would handle literally all of the company's business matters. I was hired merely to do the on/offline marketing, but my boss was convinced that I could be trusted to handle that *and* everything else. When he came on the premises, I would get the door, grab his bags, inform him on everything I had completed for the day and would eagerly ask for my next task. He would try his best not to smile, but he was thoroughly impressed with the time I was saving him simply by listening and following instructions.

I would listen to him talk about his dreams, goals and ideas, and would submit ways to help make them come into fruition. He would come up with a plan to make our next project even bigger, and I would submit money and time saving options that would benefit the company. Had I not listened to what was going through his mind, I would've blocked myself off from valuable information, which in turn would've blocked my success in the company.

There's no debating that a woman loves it when a man listens, because women love to talk. Personally, I don't have the time, energy or desire to wrack my brain trying to figure out the never-ending possibilities of what a woman wants. I find it much easier to go directly to the source and gather information. If you listen to a woman, she will give you an *idea* of what she wants, leaving you the opportunity to creatively deliver. Not taking the time to listen to your lady will result in an unsatisfied woman because you didn't take the time to listen and cater to her needs.

No matter whether it's a job, a child, or a woman, there will always be a vast untapped mountain of truth and valuable information waiting for you to break it down. You won't have to break it down by force, all you have to do is be willing to go through the process called *listening*. It will show in your eyes, body language and overall attitude how interested you are in what another person has to say. With the right attitude you can unlock the mysteries that continue to boggle your mind. With the wrong attitude, you will continue to block yourself off from life altering, life changing information.

Learn How To Share

The world can be a cold, hard and lonely place for a man, so it's natural to sometimes feel as if you are alone. It seems as though you've literally had to fight for every position, every opportunity and every ounce of success you've ever had. Over time you've become respected as a man, as a professional and as a great friend to many. Sometimes when we climb mountains, we get so high up that we forget about the people down below who have been cheering us on the entire time. You may think you've gotten to where you are on your own, but there is always someone that deserves credit for helping you along the way. Giving back and paying forward are great ways to share some of your wealth of love, knowledge and resources to others.

When I was a kid, I looked forward to my birthday because I knew that my Uncle Kermit would send me a birthday card with some cash in it. My birthday is on December 18th, exactly one week before Christmas, so I didn't expect too much from my parents on my birthday. When the cash came rolling in my brothers would hover over to see how much was inside. It was normally somewhere around $10 which seemed like an awful lot of money at the time. I was torn because I wanted to keep the money all to myself, but I knew I would want some of their birthday money when the time came.

My brother Shane's birthday was on January 6th so I knew I'd be paying him a visit VERY soon. My younger brother Joshua's birthday had just passed on

November 17th and he'd be fine simply with a piece of candy. My older brother Travis' birthday was ALL the way in July and he would always claim that he's "saving" his money when his cash came. He was a few years older than I was so he would always get a little bit more cash. At the end of the day, they would remind me "Ok, I'm going to remember this when my birthday comes around" and I would reluctantly fork over a dollar.

Now, I'm all about sharing, really I am, it was my brothers that I was concerned about. That's my story and I'm sticking to it. :p I wanted them to be just as willing to part with some of their birthday money as I was with mine. After all, *my* world would be a much better place if I could arrange residual income on their birthday money. lol To this day we are still learning how to share our time, energy, efforts and resources.

It's funny because *sharing* is something that most parents emphasize when they bring their children around other children. We want so badly to have everything to ourselves, not realizing the relationships we will build through sharing. It's a good thing we have our parents or some sort of guidance to show us a better way than what we know. Otherwise, we'll be stuck in our "Mine! Mine! Mine!" phase, but worst of all stuck there alone. No one wants to build with a selfish person because it will cost them too much and gain them too little.

Life is about building relationships and leaving behind legacies, and the more you share your resources with others, the greater the relationship will be and the greater legacy you'll have. I always tell people that if you're good at something, always do it for free until enough people respect and acknowledge that you're good at it. That's what networking is all about, figuring out a way to work together, save each other time, energy, effort and money and propel the relationship. Through combining your resources, you'll be able to maximize your profitability.

Not everything is always about numbers. Years ago when I first started out with photography, I was interested in mastering my craft before asking for a price. I would look at my competitors work and try to figure out how they were able to create such masterful images. Some were kind enough to reveal some of their secrets while others were reluctant to do so, if they even responded at all. For the ones who shared their wisdom, we were able to start the beginning of a long-lasting professional relationship.

Through consulting with my fellow photographer friends, I discovered that I could improve my images if I used better lighting, a better camera, better models, a make-up and hair stylist and post-production. I thought to myself, "No wonder... all this time it was just me, my camera, the model, whatever light was available, and that's it". Don't get me wrong, I was able to produce great images with what I had, but what they've shared with me was advice that would help me get *better*. It would require me to outsource and bring in more people and resources to help me achieve my goals. Ultimately, this would allow me to increase my knowledge of new lighting, new camera equipment, as well as meet new people.

What's was great about this experience was that there were models, make-up artists, hair stylists and even photo editors who were facing similar issues. They too wanted to enhance their portfolios; while what they already had was good, they wanted to make it even better. For the model, having a professional make-up artist, hair stylist, photographer and photo editor would mean more bookings. For the make-up artist and hair stylist, the opportunity to work with an industry standard model, photographer and photo editor would enhance their portfolios and also increase booking. And the same for the photo editor and myself, we were all able to benefit from our combined resources. All we had to do was be willing to give our time, and if need be combine our resources to rent a studio.

We did more for each other than just create beautiful images; we built a relationship. As individuals, we struggled with creating a masterpiece, but together we each added our own much-needed pieces to the puzzle. We've created a circle of trust, a network, a family of resources that we could invite others to be a part of. At any point, we could diversify our portfolios simply by swapping out one photographer, one model, one make-up artist/hair stylist, or one photo editor for another. The idea was to share what we brought to the table and encourage other people to do the same.

When you think of the most successful companies in the world, (i.e. Coca Cola, McDonald's, Nike, etc.) you will find that they didn't make it to the top on their own. That would be exhausting, to come up with all of the ideas, all of the money and all of the ways to make it happen. Instead they build partnerships and include other people, other companies and other brands to help propel them into the position that they want the company to be in. Could you imagine me trying to do the photography, the hair, the make-up, the set-design and the postproduction all by myself? That would leave me little to no time to do the actual photo shoot.

By sharing your knowledge, time and resources with others you will put yourself in a much better position to advance. In fact, whenever you're looking to build a relationship with someone, the first thing you should try to figure out is "How can I help". If you go into a situation offering to help, people will be more likely to ask you "What are your strengths". You can get into almost any and every door simply by offering to be of service, yet many people miss this opportunity because of selfish reasons. Once you're in the door, you'll have the opportunity to showcase your skills, and since you're not being paid for it, there will be less pressure on you to *not* mess up.

You don't get a 2nd chance to make a 1st impression, and by offering your services, you've just left a mark that says you are charitable as you are resourceful. These are great qualities to start a relationship off with and they will never be forgotten. In today's times, many people are so reluctant to announce their skills, or showcase their talents because they're afraid that someone might ask them to be of service. Offering to share your expertise is simply another way for you to practice. If you're truly as good as you think or say you are, the people you've shared your gifts with will gladly refer you.

In order for you to truly benefit from sharing your time, gifts, talents and resources with others, you must first change your attitude towards it. You must change your attitude towards people and think of the change you'll inspire in others. Sometimes other people won't take a step forward until you do. Some people have some of the most amazing talents and they bury them because they haven't experienced the power of giving. Sharing isn't solely about what you give; it's also about *how* you give it.

In a relationship, the success will depend on your ability to give because it's a partnership. When you're single, you're *independent*, but in a relationship you're *interdependent*. That means you no longer have to do everything on your own, you have a partner who is there to help, but that partner is also looking for reciprocity. Share your time, share your resources, share your thoughts, share your feelings, and share anything that will bring you closer together. If you're not ready to share all of these things with someone, simply spare them by remaining single.

A partnership is about more than one force coming together to improve their quality of life. If you're able to do great things on your own, you'll be amazed at what you'll be able to do together. The more you know about yourself, the more value you'll be able to add to others. If you see something that is missing from someone's life that you are able to provide, that's your opportunity to fill that void. Keeping everything you know, everything you own and everything desire to yourself will only leave you by yourself.

Learn How To Dress

As you grow and mature, so should your wardrobe. When you're a child, it's cool to wear sneakers that light up, jeans with all types of crazy designs and hats with your favorite cartoon characters on them, but when you're an adult, not so much. The first thing people will notice when they see you is your attire, so give them a good show. From your hair-cut, to your outfit to your shoes, be sure to present yourself as the person you want to be known and remembered as.

Growing up in a house full of boys, I didn't know WHAT to wear. I was too busy trying to dress like my older brothers. For years, my mom would try to nip that in the bud by dressing us all alike, but as we grew older, we wanted our own unique style. If my older brothers said it was cool, then it *was*, and if they didn't I would still rock it with pride, defending it to the death. I had the good fortune of getting many hand-me-downs because I was much smaller than my older brothers. Once they grew out of it, I gladly stepped into it.

Finally, I got to incorporate my older brother's style into my wardrobe, which was constantly growing. Even if the clothes didn't fit me, I would find a way to make it work. We had lots of different ways to make our clothes last because we had to. The only time we went clothes' shopping was during back to school season. For the rest of the year, we knew not to ask my mom to shop for anything! We had clothes from the previous year that we would reuse until they couldn't be used anymore.

We could cut jeans into shorts, dye blue jeans black, or bleach them white; whatever we had to do to make them last. We didn't have a lot of clothes, but no matter what, we were always sharp. Especially on Sundays, my mom didn't play when it came to our "Sunday outfits". We were "suited and booted" each and every Sunday, all dressed in the same style of suits. People always thought that my older brothers and I were triplets, and I would say, "No, it's just the suits". lol

There was a lot of pressure growing up in the NY area to dress a certain way. For us, the latest fashions were Air Force One's, Timberland boots, NY fitted caps and the big puffy Goose coats. There was nothing particularly special about these things; they simply were apart of our culture at the time. And since everybody else had them, *we* wanted them. My mom never succumbed to the pressures of buying into the propaganda; she would simply stick to her regular once a year shopping habits. Thank God she did, otherwise I would be a total wreck trying to keep up with name brands and such.

In fact, I didn't even know what a name brand was until I was in the fourth grade. I remember because I had gotten my very first pair of Nike's. I was attending a new school, and someone made a comment saying "Oh I see you've got name brands". I smiled and was like "Yea!" but in my head, I thought, "What in the world is a name brand". Prior to this instance, name brands meant nothing to me, I was simply happy to have a new pair of sneakers on my feet that I liked. After school I asked my older brother Shane, "What is a name brand" and he gave me the answer.

Apparently, having name brand clothes and shoes was some sort of stamp of approval amongst the people who thought they were cool. From that point on, I made a point to request name brand shoes when we went shopping. Of course, when we went shopping the name brands cost much more than regular sneakers, which resulting in me settling for a pair of sneakers that had the Nike brand, but was as ugly as sin. I didn't have any clothes to match it, they weren't diverse or could work with any occasion and it didn't add any value to my life. I had been sucked into the vicious cycle that many of us have become victims to.

When you're a kid, you're not concerned with the cost of things, because it's not coming out of your pocket. All you can think about is making a good impression on your friends at school. You don't want the cool kids to pick on you because of your poor style of dress or worse, being laughed at by the girls. You want to feel good about yourself, and please others at the same time. During the early stages of your life, finding your own identity will be one of the greatest challenges you will face in your life.

As you grow older and mature, your values will begin to change, as should your style of dress. Your goals are higher and your network larger, your vision clearer and your confidence stronger. Over time you've learned how to value the person who goes into the clothes and not merely the clothes themselves. You've told yourself over and over how valuable you are, how intelligent you are and how good looking you are. And then as you begin to dress yourself, you tell yourself "I look even *better* with these clothes".

Your style of dress will change dramatically depending on where you are in life. I've had the good fortune of living in New York, New Jersey, Atlanta, and Texas; and each state had their own unique style. New York and New Jersey had very similar taste, however Atlanta and Texas was a whole other world. In Atlanta the boys would actually tuck their jeans into their socks; strange, but it was *their* thing. In Texas, the boys would use a ridiculously excessive amount of starch on their jeans; very strange, but it was *their* thing.

No matter where I've lived, I tried my best to adjust based on a number of things: who I was, where I was and the people who were around me. I wanted to "do as the Romans did" while I was in Atlanta, but also maintain my New York swag. I tried my best to hold onto my New York accent, and would occasionally tuck my socks into my jeans. While in Texas, I literally used an entire can of starch on my jeans and still could not get it right. I was losing myself trying to fit in; it did nothing for my budget, nothing for my credibility and nothing for my peace of mind.

In my junior year of high school, I transferred to Saint Anthony high school in Jersey City, NJ where I immediately joined the popular basketball program. Thank God we had a school uniform that we wore everyday because I did not want to have to explain to my teammates why I was tucking my jeans into my socks or super creasing my pants. I would've ruined any possibility of a friendship with the guys, and I could forget about getting a date with the girls. Even with our uniforms the guys would figure out a stylish way to finagle their individuality. It wasn't enough to wear khakis; you weren't cool until you got the ones with *pockets* in them.

After graduation, I moved back to Texas and attended Texas Wesleyan University, but I refused to crease my jeans. "I'm a New Yorker", I thought to myself "and I will stick to my Air Force One's, Timberland boots, baggy clothes and NY fitted caps. I was the MAN during that period of my life, but still growing. All of the girls at college loved the way I dressed, my NY swag, and my NY accent. Down south they treat New Yorkers like we're celebrities!

One of the problems that I faced when I moved back to NY was, there was nothing special or unique about the way I dressed, my accent or my "NY swag". Everyone and their mother had it! It was so bad, that you could hardly recognize a lot of the people because they all looked the same. The same Air Force One's, Timberland boots, White T-Shirt, blue NY fitted cap and bubble coat (if it was winter). I was a statistic and it was entirely my fault; I didn't know how to dress. Even my long braids were a fashion fad that was getting old.

I tried to apply to a job in NY and they said "No braids". I loved my braids, but I was not going to let a hairstyle get in the way of my future. I remember the day, it was June 5, 2005 when I cut my braids and it felt good letting go. I felt like a grown man, and not only did I let go of the braids, I let go of the baggy clothes, Air Force One's, Timberland Boots, and bubble coats. My new closet consisted of shoes, slacks, blazers, suits, ties, button down shirts, sweaters, vests and overcoats that actually fit me. I've managed to completely reinvent myself by doing away with childish things and started walking, talking and dressing like a man. I wanted to look the way I felt, so I did away with everything that made me look like a boy running around the streets of Brooklyn and started to dress like a man who runs New York.

Sometimes in order to change your life you have to change your ways; this will require a complete destruction of your old self and a reconstruction of your new self. *Now*, when you walk into a room, people will want to know who you are, what you do and even where you shop. Women will be attracted because you dress and carry yourself like a man of purpose, an effective leader, and a role model. You will spark interest in others which will result in exclusive invitations into their social circles simply because you appear as if you belong. Finally, you will feel better about yourself as a man because now you've now done more than simply make an adjustment to your wardrobe, you've made an adjustment to your attitude, and an even greater adjustment to your life.

Learn How To Cook

There's nothing like coming home to a nice home-cooked meal prepared by someone you love. You can tell the dish was made with love because they took their time to make sure that the flavors were just right, cooked to perfection and *then* served. Every cook who takes pride in their work can't wait to hear that "Mmmm" sound after someone takes their first bite because *that* lets them know that their mission was accomplished. Food is without a doubt the way to a man's heart, but guess what? Women love to eat too! You'll find that amongst many other things, a woman loves a man who knows how to cook.

If you don't know how to cook, learn how. It's important for any man to know how to work his way around the kitchen not just for the sake of his lady, but for his *own* sake. Not only will learning how to cook fill your belly, but it will also build your character. Everything you learn can be taught, and cooking is one of those things that never goes out of style. You can make an evening of it, invite friends over for a pot luck, have one friend chop this, another boil that, while the others peel something else. Invite over a nutritionist or a professional chef to give you some pointers on how to make cooking healthy, easy and fun.

If you have children, there will be nights and days where you will have to prepare a meal for them, and it helps to be prepared ahead of time. You'll be surprised how easy it is to prepare and cook meals even with limited supplies once you have the skills. Most kids want fast food (i.e. Cheeseburgers, pizza, chicken nuggets, etc). You can use this information to not only prepare a meal that you know they'll love, but you can also include them. You see now, you've created the perfect bonding opportunity for you and your family. You can show them how to properly season, the right temperature to cook at, and also use a timer to make sure nothing gets overcooked.

Kids love to be included in family activities that are fun, and cooking is certainly one of them. I remember as a kid, my mom would bake cakes, and my brothers and I would always volunteer to help. There were so many things we could do like crack the eggs, pour in the milk/water/oil/batter, and mix everything together. There were 4 boys in the house so we had to share the responsibilities, which was another great thing we learned. We got a chance to set the oven and put the cake inside and when it was finished, we would all help put icing on the cake. Our favorite part was when we got to lick the bowl. ☺

My mother knew how much we loved those special moments so she would include us as often as possible. After awhile, my mother no longer needed to micromanage us in the kitchen; we had baked cakes so many times, we could do it with our eyes closed. We would talk, laugh, sing and dance in the kitchen as we prepared a delicious cake that we would later enjoy. My mom could've very well made the cake on her own and would've gotten finished with it 5 times faster without us, but it wasn't about the cake. My mother was creating an environment where we could enjoy one another's company.

It's a good thing she knew how to cook because my stepfather's idea of a home-cooked meal was "Franks and Beans". Anytime my mother went out of town, we would all look at each other like "What are we going to eat" lol. We had a skillet that plugged into the wall, and when my step-dad cooked chicken inside of it, it would make this delicious crispy chicken and skin that we loved. That was the extent of his cooking and we would soon resort to "Oodles Of Noodles". We were young boys at the time, so we would make it work for the few days my mom would go away. When my mom finally returned, we would run to her and beg her never to leave again as if she were Jesus!

We missed my mom's home cooked meals dearly and we were ever so happy to have her back. My step-dad missed the opportunity to bond with us over that weekend probably because his dad missed it with him. This is a cycle that can be broken and should be broken. Rolling up your sleeves and getting down in the kitchen isn't a job just for women, it's a job for anyone who wants to have a decent meal. While you're single, you should be developing these skills on your own, which will add tremendous value to your relationship when you have one. In fact, you may even find love while shopping for groceries; there are plenty of single and eligible candidates right in your local market.

Eating out can get quite expense, not to mention you'll have no creative control over what actually goes into your food. You'll save a ton of money by going grocery shopping, preparing your own meals and eating in. You'll also learn a lot about yourself during this process, like the kind of foods you like, foods you'd love to try, and dishes you enjoy preparing the most. You can create your own menu, perfect your signature dishes and who knows, one day you may even write a cookbook or become a chef. There are so many wonderful possibilities that can stem from you learning how to cook.

Eating is something that no one can live without, so by learning how to supply this demand, you can make yourself indispensable in that area. Any woman who knows me knows that if she cooks for me, she's my NEW best friend. At my church, they have a ministry for the men called "The Front Liners", and at our bi-monthly meetings we talk about God, life and relationships. I know what you're thinking, "What's in it for me?" In addition to the food for the soul that we receive at these meetings, they also provide food for the body, and that has managed to pack the house every time. It's not rocket science, it's simply common knowledge that people are more likely to show up at places where there will be food.

Have you ever hosted a Thanksgiving dinner for your friends and family at your home? You would if you knew how to cook! It's fun to entertain other people with your gifts, however it's impossible to give out something that you are without. Don't be ashamed to go online, ask a friend, or turn to a family member for cooking lessons. I'm sure if you provided the food and ingredients that they would love the idea of coming over to teach you how to prepare your favorite dishes. Give it a try, plan a day in advance and invite over a few of your closest family members, friends and relatives. You will come out of the deal will all sorts of delicious dishes and plenty of leftovers, but most of all, you'll have a great bonding experience with your loved ones.

The internet is filled with great recipes on any and everything you could possibly imagine. Subscribe to your favorite YouTube channels and stay updated on their latest creations. There are plenty of other men just like you who feel they don't have the time, the energy or the skills to cook a decent meal. Once you make a conscious effort to make your cooking ideas become a reality, you can take pride of showing the world otherwise. Post pictures and recipes on your social media networks, inspire people who are or were just like you, and show that *anyone* can cook.

My grandfather Hayward C. Bostock was a great chef; he studied culinary arts and it showed. As kids, we loved going to his house so that we could spend quality time with our grandparents, but what we also looked forward to was their cooking. There was never a time where they didn't have a fancy meal laid out for us; lamb chops, stuffing, collard greens, mac n cheese, you name it! We would pray over the food, sit, eat and talk about whatever was on our minds. After our hearts were content and our bellies were full, we would reminisce on all of the previous delicious meals that came from their kitchen.

At first, we would assume that it was my grandmother who cooked all of the meals because traditionally the women would do the cooking. It was to our amazement that in fact it was my grandfather who did a lot of the cooking. That was a proud moment for us, it gave us a glimpse of the type of man my grandfather was. It showed us that he wasn't too proud to prepare a meal for his lady, even in his old age. They had been married for about 50 years, and although they had gotten old, he kept things fresh and new in the kitchen.

When it comes to your relationship, preparing a meal for your lady will open up many doors. First, it will open up the doors to her heart; making the time to cater to your woman is a heart-felt gesture. It will open up the doors of conversation, for there will be many flavors, colors and textures to talk about. Not to mention the relaxed environment you'll create to talk about even more important matters. Now that you've shown how much you care without being prompted to do so, she'll feel inspired to do the same.

Adding this great quality to your life will make a remarkable difference within yourself, amongst your family/friends and with your lady. Women find men who cook to be very attractive, and you don't want to miss out on the opportunity to fall into *that* category. If the both of you don't know how to cook, don't fret because that is yet another opportunity to bond *if* she is willing to learn. If you both already know how to cook, even better; take turns preparing meals for one another, and also join forces and create great meals together. Teamwork makes the dream work!

Ordering out is easy, taking the time to plan and figure out what to eat, how to make it, and then putting it into action can be easy too. You simply have to practice and get in the habit of doing it, and after awhile it will feel natural. Like everything else in life, you won't know how to do something until you do it. Sometimes you won't have access to hands on training, or an adviser to walk you through, so have faith in your abilities and you'll be just fine. You'll make many mistakes on this journey, but you'll also make many corrections. And the best part about learning how to cook is the tasting. Enjoy!

Chapter 3:

Understanding A Woman

Know The Value Of A Woman

One of God's greatest creations was a woman. She can give birth, love and nurture a child, excel at work, and take care of a home and everyone in it all without even breaking a sweat. And this is merely scratching the service of a woman's greatness! The best part about valuing the woman who is a part of your life is that when you acknowledge her greatness, she will be more willing to do great things for you. She'll give birth to your children with pride, she'll take care of the home and everyone in it, and she'll do it all with a smile on her face.

With men, everything is black and white, cut and dry, plain and simple. With women there is always a gray area, a wider color spectrum or a complexity to every situation. That's what makes a woman so amazing! Not only do they see things differently than you do, but they look at how you see things and imagine something greater that could come of it. Take lunch for example, you may be ok with a bowl of Ramen noodles, but a woman of substance will come and produce a more healthy and balanced meal that will not only taste good but will also give you the nutritional value that your body needs.

A woman can help upgrade you from a good man to a great one if you allow her to. Once a woman has decided that she wants to pour into your life, all you have to do is pour back into hers. Just like you, a woman wants to be loved, valued and appreciated and she takes great pride in being with a man who gives her that sort of security. If a woman doesn't feel secure in who you are and the value you add to the relationship, it's only a matter of time before she decides to end the relationship. If you want a woman to stay, give her hope; if you want a woman to leave, give her doubt.

When it comes to catering to a woman in a relationship, try to think of it as a business partnership. In order for the partnership to work, you both have to bring value to the relationship. In addition, you both have to acknowledge and respect the value that is being brought into the relationship. You each will have your own individual strengths and weaknesses, and that's the beauty of coming together, to empower one another and help each other overcome those weaknesses through your individual strengths. If your lady doesn't feel as though you are supportive of her goals, or you take no interest in helping her grow, or you don't compliment her strengths, then she won't see the value in being in a relationship with you.

Instead, try and remember who you are, why you were chosen, and the position you signed up for. If you've signed up to be significant in a woman's life, it is your job to have value within yourself, see value in her, and add value to her life. A woman looks to her man to compliment her beauty, skills and resourcefulness, and it's as simple as saying "Babe, you are amazing!" These four simple words will make a world of difference in your woman's life and will inspire her to continue doing great things for herself, for others, and certainly for you. Be a source for love, joy and happiness, and she will never want to go a day without connecting with you.

One thing that many men struggle with is being sensitive to other people's feelings. If you're going to be successful with a woman, this is a practice you will have to learn how to master. Women are naturally very sensitive and emotional beings, and that is never going to change. Being sensitive and emotional is a human thing, not just a woman thing, it's just that many men have yet to tap into their emotional and sensitive side. That's where a woman comes in, to help bring out the softer side of a man.

When you think about it, women are like magicians, they can make amazing things happen right before your eyes. Some of the roughest, toughest and angriest men you'll ever meet can be broken down by a woman. That in itself has tremendous value that we as men must be thankful for, because in all honesty, no man wants to constantly have his guard up and act rough, tough and angry all the time. This is an act that a lot of men put on to protect their hearts, image or street credibility. It yields no peace of mind to have a 24/7 chip on your shoulder and live your life without love, so for their amazing talents and abilities, we must be grateful for the power of love that dwells inside of a woman.

The power of a belief system will take you to unbelievable new heights. If you don't believe me, give your woman a task and let her know that you have faith that she can do it. Go ahead and try it, ask her to put together a business plan, coordinate a spectacular event, or prepare an exquisite dish she's never made before. Knowing that you believe in her is all the motivation she will ever need to get the job done. The value was always there, she simply needed someone to help bring it out of her. That someone is you!

If you spend the entire duration of your relationship bringing out the value of your woman, you'll never get bored with your relationship. Push her in different directions helping her reach her goals, pull her away from danger and into safety because you care, lead her into prosperity because she means that much to you. The key to staying relevant in any relationship is solely based on the value you bring into the relationship. You make yourself indispensable if you are able to master the art of constantly inspiring your partner to be great.

The value of a woman isn't solely about what she's done in her past, but also about what she is a currently doing in the present and what she aspires to do in the future. Sometimes after experiencing the struggled of our past, we decide that our past isn't the place we want to be. Meeting *you* could possibly be the best thing that has ever happened to your woman because you give her hope. Finally, a man who loves himself, loves others and by the grace of God loves her. This feeling of love can have a life changing impact on anyone and can shift a person's values in an instant.

No matter who you are, where you're from, or what you do, everyone's circumstances is subject to change once you find love. Sometimes it's hard for a person to see their own value when they're not surrounded by people who have values. When a person changes their surroundings and associates with positive people and things, it eventually rubs off on them. In your lifetime you will meet many different women from different backgrounds and they all have a past. Just remember that even though they have a past, that you too have one.

One of the best ways to make corrections in life is through making mistakes. There's always room for improvement, and even when you fall short, you are still valuable. Not every woman comes from a home with parents who teach great morals, values and principles, and for the one's who do, not every women takes heed. As a man, it is your job to lead a woman, no matter how dark her past may be, if you choose to be with her, take her by the hand and guide her into the light. Hopefully by the time you're ready to search for a woman, you will have already found the light, which will make your leadership path that much easier.

Being in a relationship is a job in and of itself. If you're going to give a woman a position in your life, give it to her because you see her potential and intend to help her reach it. It's easy to get into a relationship with someone who already "has it all" because there's no work to be done. Be careful when choosing a woman who is "already made" because her expectations may exceed your capabilities and when your usefulness expires, so will the relationship. Women get bored very easily, so if you intend to keep up, you must first work on yourself, discover what your true value is and connect on a spiritual level with a woman who will appreciate the value that you bring to the table.

Be sure not to ignore this step because your own individual value will have a great impact on the value of the women you attract. For example, you can't ask for a rich/fit woman if you're not a rich/fit man. Become the total package and you'll find it easier to attract the total package. The total package means that you are spiritually, emotionally, physically and financially stable. Having these 4 basic things adds value to your life, and seeing these things come into fruition will show a woman how much you value yourself.

Self-love is a prerequisite to any relationship because it's a reflection of your capacity to love and care for others. When you don't love yourself, you'll begin to view women in the same light that you subconsciously view yourself (i.e. Unworthy, lacking in value). It's hard to see value in others when you don't have it or see it in yourself, and it's easy to point the finger at others when you're afraid to take accountability for your own actions. Once you've taken the time to love and value yourself, it's like removing a pair of foggy goggles from your eyes, you can see people for who they really are, as opposed to labeling them according to what they do or have done.

The value of *your* woman will have a lot to do with the value in *you*. It's your choice who to engage in conversation, date, marry and/or have kids with, so be sure to evaluate your values system before making a life-time commitment to avoid a life-time nightmare. No matter how much or how little a woman values herself, it's your job as a man to either love her or leave her alone. Lead the relationship into prosperity, encourage your lady's strengths, and show appreciation for all of her contributions and she will continue to follow.

Women Love To Talk

One of the most important keys to a successful relationship is communication. When it comes to communication though, it's important that you understand the audience you are communicating with. As men, we can get away with a hand shake, a head nod, or some other type of body language when dealing with one other, however when dealing with a woman, they value a man who knows how to articulate his thoughts and feelings more so through words. Sure, there will be times when she'll be able to pick up certain underlying meanings that are associated with your actions, however having an actual conversation discussing the topic at hand will help put her mind at ease which will in turn bring peace back into the relationship and in the home.

A relationship is about compromise so if you're looking for a woman who has substance and will add great value to your life, you should also aspire to add value to hers. Before going into a relationship, you must remove all selfish thoughts and consider the feelings of your partner. For a woman, talking about feelings, expressing emotions, and going over details comes second nature. They haven't been trained to suppress their thoughts, hide their emotions, and communicate through codes the same way us men have, so we can't look for them to speak the same language as we do. Think of communicating with a woman as an opportunity to learn a foreign language; pay attention, take notes and learn how to speak in a way that a woman will understand.

A woman doesn't have the ability to read your mind, nor should she have to. In a relationship, there has to be clear communication. Communication isn't simply about a message being sent from a sender to a receiver. It's also about whether or not the message was clearly understood, and you'll know whether or not the message was clearly understand based on her feedback. If the message you're sending is being received in a way that the sender can't understand, then all you're doing is creating *noise*. Where there is noise, miscommunication and misunderstandings will follow, not to mention a great deal of frustration and valuable time wasted.

A great way to avoid having noise in communication with your lady is to take the time to understand her language; both the way she speaks and the way she listens. It's worth it to seek understanding in the area of communication because without healthy communication in a relationship, the relationship will eventually fall apart. It will be like talking to a brick wall and vice versa and yelling "You're not listening to me" and the wall isn't showing any signs of emotion or concern in response. After a while, either the wall is going to break down or you will, but the whole idea of a relationship is to keep everyone and everything together.

A woman understands that being a man is rough, it's hard and there's a lot riding on your shoulders. What she further wants to understand is how you're dealing with it on the inside. She cares not only about the shell of a man, but also about the heart of the man. When she asks you "Hey babe, how was your day", she's asking out of concern, not to annoy you. She's concerned about the quality of your life and the details of your day because she looks to you for protection, for you to provide and for you to lead her into prosperity. It gives her a greater sense of security knowing that her man has peace of mind.

As a man, it may be difficult to allow yourself to be vulnerable and express your innermost thoughts and feelings to someone. This is all a part of being a man. It's ok to talk about the things that make you happy, sad, excited and even angry. Holding onto these mixed emotions will be like constantly throwing things into a volcano that's just waiting to erupt. It's therapeutic to express yourself in a positive and constructive way to help relieve any stress you may have within. The best part is that a woman of substance will have already mastered the ability to listen and advise on matters pertaining to the heart.

Communication is great for both parties because you get a chance to listen to and learn more about each other, and you also get the opportunity to be heard. It's better to first come to one another and talk about your differences than to outsource them. You can never run out of things to say to one another, you simply have to create the space and opportunity to embark in meaningful dialogue with one another. For example, you can talk about there day at work/school, what they'd like to eat for lunch/dinner, planning a vacation or date night, or simply catering to one another's individual desires.

A woman loves it when you show her that you love her, but she equally adores it when you tell her. Words have tremendous power and when you speak things into existence, they become real. For a man, you might be just fine if a woman never says the words "I love you" but remember, women value different things. Hearing you say the words means something to her and she looks for you to express yourself in a way that makes her feel comfortable, even if it's uncomfortable for you. It's a small price to pay for a quality woman of substance, but it's better to pay this small price than to lose her for not showing her how much you care.

A woman wants you to make her feel as though she is a priority, not a convenience. Anyone can send a "Good morning beautiful, how are you?" text message. It shows more value when you pick of the phone, call and refer to her by name and say "Hi (fill in name), how are you?". When communicating with your guy friends, feel free to send a brief/impersonal text message with short hand, jargon and ambiguity, but when associating with a woman, be gentle. Chivalry will get you as far as you want to go with a woman; all you have to do is be consistent.

When you pick up the phone and call a woman, you are doing more than having just a regular conversation; you are showing her that you value her enough to make time to talk to her. And by making time to talk to her, you have premeditated topics of interest that might bring the two of you closer together. A woman loves a man who has a plan and she's dying to see where your mind is prepared to take her. Neglect to pick up the phone and call and it will have the opposite effect. It will show her how little you value her and reluctant you are to include her into your schedule, how little creativity you have, and how ineffectively you are able to lead her.

Your desire to communicate and your ability to communicate are two totally different things. Anyone with the ability to communicate has enough creativity in them to come up with topics of discussions that will engage an audience and keep them entertained. Choosing *not* to reveals more about your character and your ability to lead than you know. In effective leadership, one must learn how to be slow to speak and quick to listen, but equally efficient in both. A woman not only is interested in listening to your heart's desires, but she also wants a man who is ready, willing and able to listen to hers.

Ignoring a woman's thoughts and feelings is a great way to lose her. Women have what I like to call a "Grace Period" before she takes extreme action. At first she'll beg and plead for you to talk to her, then she'll turn to family members and female friends, and then finally to male friend/admirers who are always ready to be "supportive" in her time of need. Better to talk to your lady, pay attention to her thoughts, concerns and desires and cater to them to the best of your abilities. In other words, take care of home.

Women are used to men trying to short change them, degrade them and get something for nothing, so when you show that you are special, she'll treat you as though you are special. If all of the other contenders are sending mass texts, send her a letter in the mail. Not only will you spark a higher level of interest from the woman, but you will immediately stand out amongst everyone else without even trying.

A Woman Will Submit To You When You Submit To God

Women are so amazing; they're beautiful, smart, resourceful and add tremendous value to the world in so many ways. In today's times, more and more women are challenging themselves to do the impossible and are proving to be quite successful at it. They are opening up businesses, running multi-million dollar corporations, raising children and looking good while doing it. No longer are women of substance confining themselves to a man's kitchen or bedroom, they are out conquering the world. Somewhere out there she believes that there is a man who is strong enough, wise enough and loving enough to settle her down, but until then she will remain "Single By Design".

Being single is the thing you do when you are establishing/finding yourself and/or when you haven't met someone who meets your standards. You may not like it, but being single by design sounds like a genius plan to me. There's no sense in a woman who loves God, is thriving in her career, being of service in her community and being a great friend to many to settle for *just* you if you're not offering anything greater. In order to get a woman to settle for you, that's exactly what you need, evidence that you have access to something greater. The way to achieve that is by showing her that you are led by truth, and influenced by love.

Often times a man believes that a woman is obligated to follow his lead simply because he is a man, and I'm here to tell you that no woman of substance is going to let that fly. You have to prove to her that you have good leadership otherwise you'll find yourself walking alone. Life is too short to waste valuable time accompanying someone on a journey that has no destination. Women of substance know very well how simple we men are; all we need is food, sex and peace of mind and we're *good*. Once we get what we want, we usually aren't remotely interested in catering to their needs.

Since this is so and has been proven countless times over, a woman must protect her investment and require you to do more in order to have her hand. Your words aren't enough; she wants to see you put things into action. You've been there before, a woman will make you believe that there is hope for romance, will watch you spend your time and money, and then leave you hanging. In hindsight you're thinking "I should've required XYZ before spending so much time, energy, effort and money". And you're absolutely right, your time and resources has value too, and it's up to you to place value on it.

There are some women out there who will sell themselves short just so that they can say they have a man, but that's not the woman you want. She'll make you feel better about your shortcomings, and compensate for them in any way that she can, not because she loves you, but because she's lonely. You'll waste valuable time in this relationship because it's not based on truth; the both of you are in denial. She'll submit just enough to keep you around, but not enough to keep you moving forward. Her strength comes from your weakness, and it won't benefit her to empower you to reach your goals.

Once you reach your goals, you will no longer need her, because there was never anything truly special about her to begin with. She was convenient for the time being, she made you feel comfortable about your situation, and over time you grew complacent. Over time, she's learned everything about you and will use that information as her excuse not to submit. For example, "You don't pay any bills" or "You don't do any handy work around the house" or "You can't afford to take me out". Now, the relationship feels like a prison because neither one of you are looking for anything better, yet you're miserable with each other.

In a woman's heart, she knows whether or not you are a man who will love her and do right by her, sometimes she denies those feelings and continues on with the relationship. She's hoping that one day you will be a better man and miraculously start caring more about the relationship. She'll try her best to dumb down her brilliance just to make you feel more like a man, but after a while that gets exhausting. Not to mention, you know as a man that you should be doing better and that what she's doing for you is pathetic. You'll be just itching to get yourself in a better position so that you can throw it back in her face.

Well that certainly is no way to get a woman to submit to you because a woman's willingness to submit will be motivated by *your* attitude. Your attitude towards people, money, time and things will have great influence over a woman's decision to associate with you. You could be the richest and most successful man in the world, and it would mean nothing to a woman if your attitude were poor. But show a woman that you love God, you love life and you love her and you love God and she'll follow you to the end of the earth. Love conquers all, which is why it should always be the foundation of your relationship.

When we take into account what it means for a woman to submit to a man, know that it does not mean that you are the boss of her. Submission means *to yie*ld! We all can recall when we were students in school, we would come into our classrooms and we would focus our attention on the teacher. In a classroom, there has to be order in order to get the most value out of the experience. The teacher is there to teach us based on her knowledge and experience, and we are there to learn from him/her.

Since they have taken the time to master their field of study, we trust that they are capable of leading us into prosperity. We don't assume the role of the teacher because we hope to learn all he/she knows. We also want the teacher to be open to questions, comments and suggestions while still taking the lead. The teacher isn't the boss of us, she's merely there to help us learn and grow. Throughout the school year, his/her goal is to help us become better than we were when we started.

If we as students don't submit to our teachers, we miss the opportunity to learn and grow. But also, the teacher must remember that in order to keep our attention and earn our respect is through their attitude. They must treat us with love, dignity and respect; otherwise we will lose respect for them. And we all know what happens in a classroom when the student doesn't respect the teacher, and refuses to submit; they cause a disturbance. Not only does the disturbance affect the teacher's ability to teach, but it also affect the student's ability to learn.

In the end, both parties walk away empty handed. Their attitude towards one another has ruined the opportunity for growth. When it comes to growing in a relationship, it has to be a two-way street. You can't ask someone to yield to you if you are unwilling to yield to anyone else. When I was growing up, it seemed as if grown ups did not like to be challenged, the only possible rebuttal they could come up with was "Stay in a child's place" or "Respect your elders" or simply "Shut your mouth". They wanted to have the authority over you, but refused to reveal *their* source that gave them the authority to "lay down the law".

Now, I'm all for respecting elders, obeying parents, etc, but right is right and wrong is wrong and I can't just go following behind stupidity. There needs to be some *sense* behind your leadership in order for me to invest my time. As you grow into a man, you will find that many of the things your elders said was just plain baseless, and you have to find your own source of knowledge just as they did. Some people pride themselves in saying "My momma always told me…" well sometimes momma didn't have the slightest clue as to what she was talking about. This isn't to discount the wisdom bestowed upon us from our parents, but rather to encourage you to find your own way.

Times change, but principles do not. A woman should know her role in a relationship, and as a man you should too. If you don't know how to speak to a woman, you will disqualify your own self as a possible candidate. If you don't know how to cater to a woman, a woman won't want to cater to you. Everyone wants to be happy, so don't be so quick to judge a woman simply because her standards require you to do some *real* work.

A woman knows when a man has true substance as opposed to a man who merely offers suspense, and will submit only to a man who has proven himself worthy. You can show a woman that you are worthy simply by the way you live your life. She wants to be able to trust your leadership and she'll feel secure in knowing that you are led by God. When you submit to and are led by God, this gives a woman a standard to hold you to. She can now put her trust in God and follow the God that she sees in you.

If God is not in your relationship, then you shouldn't be either. God is love, and as the leader, it is your job to introduce love into the equation and set the tone. If you want your woman to go to your church, it's your job to lead her there. If you want a woman to cook, provide the tools that she needs to prepare it. If you want a woman to let you do the talking and negotiating, prove that there is power in your words. If you want a woman to stop going out all the time, give her a reason to stay home, or invite her to do things as a couple. If you want a woman to submit, you don't have to use force, simply show her the God given power you have inside of you and give her something to submit to.

A Woman Needs Romance

If you haven't noticed already, a woman of substance likes to take her time when it comes to being intimate with a man. She doesn't like to feel rushed, forced or uncomfortable when it's time to having sexual relations with a man. For a woman, the physical stimulation is merely a bonus that comes with the mental stimulation that initially gets her in the mood. They say "it's the thought that counts" and it's absolutely true! A woman wants her imagination to run wild thinking of all the things you could possibly do with one another before they actually happen.

More importantly, a woman wants to feel valued and appreciated beyond her physical appearance. She wants to know that you are ready, willing and able to invest your time, energy, effort and money into her outside of the bedroom. By showing her your appreciation through actions and in words, a woman will be more likely to open herself up to you physically and emotionally. The average woman has no problem getting a man to sleep with her, all she has to do is name the time and place. What a woman of substance truly desires is for a man to love her.

Loving a woman is what will differentiate you from the average guy. The average guy looks to come into a woman's life, take what he wants and then leaves. A man who is genuinely in love with a woman will not only have value, but he'll see value in her and then finally he'll add value to her. That's the definition of a good man. When she sees that you're different from the bad boys, she will want to do everything in her power to hold onto you. Getting a woman to be intimate isn't difficult; all you have to do is show her that you truly love her.

Women love to feel special! They want to feel as if they're the only girl in the world; above your mother, sister, daughter, female friends, co-workers and anyone else imaginable. And rightfully so; if this is your partner, she should without a doubt come first before any other woman, even mom! Have a talk with your father and he'll tell you that you should put *your* woman first before any others. When you treat a woman like she's your first lady, she'll treat you like you're her best man.

You don't want to miss the opportunity to make your lady feel special because a woman will find a way to get the attention she needs. If she's not getting it from home, you can rest assured that it will only be a matter of time before she gets it someplace else. And don't fool yourself into thinking that everything is alright simply because a woman is no longer stressing the issue. When a woman stops caring, that's an indication that she's already moved on. A woman will leave you emotionally long before she leaves you physically. You might still *see* her, but you will no longer *have* her!

When it comes to romance you must think beyond sex. The most powerful tool you have as a man is your mind. Your mind controls every other aspect of your body and has the power to influence the actions of others. Show a woman your creativity and it will remind her of who she is *to you* and how you feel about her. Every time she gets this reminder, it will motivate and inspire her to live up to her position. Give it a try, walk up to your woman and tell her "You are my Queen". It will have a great impact on her character, the company she keeps and the way she reciprocates her love to you.

Romance to a woman is about showing love, affection and compassion. Think back to when you were a child running wild at the park; it wasn't enough that your parents brought you there, you wanted them to *look* at you and pay attention to whatever it is that you were doing. It was important to you to hear your parents say the words "Good job" or "Woah! That was cool". It boosted your confidence and your esteem because they made you feel appreciated. Sure, they would've loved to talk to one another, engage with other parents or read a newspaper, but they cared so much about your well being that they made a conscious effort to take the time to validate you.

Believe it or not, women want the same special attention, love and affection that a child yearns from their parents. They want to hear you say "Dinner was excellent", "You look great", "I'm proud of you and all of your accomplishments". Why? Because it makes them feel good inside. It affirms that you see value in them, you are supportive of them and you are they are significant to you. It shows her that you are paying attention to details and that you are actively involved in her life.

Paying attention to the little things is what will open up a lot of doors for bigger things. For example, when a woman gets her hair done, give her a compliment, but *this* time go into detail. "Wow, babe your hair looks great. I love it when you wear your hair *curly*". By doing this, you're showing her that you noticed that her hair is different from before and also that you like her choice of style. This will motivate her to continue to maintain her appearance and further value your opinion.

I'll even do you one better, arrange for a day for your lady to go and get her hair done (all expense paid). Not only will she be grateful for the special treatment and return looking and feeling like a million bucks, but she'll rush back home to get *your* approval. All the while she'll be at the salon bragging to her friends about how wonderful and thoughtful you are. While she's at the salon, take care of the home, cook, clean and have a nice bubble bath waiting for her. She'll be so swept away, she won't be able to keep her hands off of you at the end of the night.

Now lets do a recap of what just happened. You took the time to schedule a hair appointment for the woman you love and got to benefit from having a fabulous looking woman by your side. You made time to clean the home you live in and cook a meal for your lady that you also get to enjoy. You ran a bubble bath for your woman and more than likely will get invited in. And finally, your woman is looking good, feeling good, smelling good and if you've played your cards right tasting good. It looks like being romantic has great benefits after all.

With only a small fraction of your time, you've been able to successfully finagle a way to do something that benefited someone else and as a result of your selflessness, it also benefited *you*. When it comes to dealing with a woman, that's what being romantic is all about. Every woman loves to have sex, but she doesn't want to have sex with a man she feels is not deserving of it. Imagine your woman is a figure inside of a thick, cold block of ice. The woman will always be there, you simply have to warm her up to you.

Most men want to jump straight to the sex without any foreplay whatsoever, and that's not the way women operate. A woman wants to be softly caressed, kissed, held and handled with care. This is why they call it a "gentle man". As opposed to the usual rough and tough routine that you would engage in with your male counter-parts or people you don't care about, a woman wants you to be gentle. Take your time, do it right and once a woman has completely warmed up to you, she'll give you the green light to accelerate at anytime and anyplace.

Understanding the psychology of a woman is the key here. If you can't tap into your sensitive side, you'll have trouble keeping a woman by your side. A woman wants a man who is tough enough to protect her, be gentle enough to care for her. She likes to see the softer side of her man behind closed doors, and strong leadership skills everywhere else. A common mistake that many men make once they get the girl is they stop competing for her love and affection. It takes a lot to keep a woman in your life, but it only takes a little to lose her.

Maintaining a relationship requires you to constantly be proactive and stay relevant. No matter how many years you've been together, it's in your best interest to make certain never to let the relationship get stale. There are plenty of things two people in a relationship can do to keep the fire going, and it's up to you to lead the way. Your passion and your desire to keep your woman happy is what will be the fuel that keeps your relationship going. Happy wife, happy life!

Keeping a woman happy isn't about spending tons of money or lots of time wooing her to no end. Women are simpler than you think; it's not that they require a lot, they simply want you to be consistent. It's no wonder she's bored. For the first few years of the relationship, every other Saturday night was date night. 5 years in, she's lucky if you're even around on Saturday night. That's no way to keep a woman happy. If you bring something to the table, the only way you should take it away is if you're offering something better. If you simply take away the excitement with no counter-offer, she's going to be constantly looking to try to get that old thing back.

Being romantic is as simple as doing the things you know she loves. For example, women love to be kissed on the forehead and held tightly. It reminds them of a love they have, had, or wish they had from their father. It's non-sexual, comforting and it gives them a greater sense of security. It doesn't cost you anything more than your time to hold your woman tight, kiss her on the forehead and tell her you love her. It won't cost you a fortune to schedule a spa day for your lady and take her out to dinner.

The actual planning process itself turns a woman on. Women love surprises and will greatly appreciative of an unsuspecting adventure orchestrated by her man. A woman loves a man with a plan, it shows his ability to lead, it shows that he cares and it shows that he is confident in himself and his abilities. All of these things matter to a woman. A woman loves it when a man is always busy taking care of his business, but is never too busy for her.

A Woman Wants A Man With A Plan

Right before the start of the New Year, I write out my goals for the upcoming year. This helps me to stay focused on my day-to-day, week-to-week and month-to-month activities throughout the year. Having a plan for what you want to do with your life is a great way and the only way to become successful. There's something about a man on a mission that every woman loves and finds extremely attractive. It shows his discipline, passion and purpose in life and that's exactly the type of man a woman wants to lead her.

For men, we are taught to be protectors and providers, and for women they are taught to be nurturers. In order to properly balance a relationship, both parties have to know their roles and play their roles. It's unfortunate, but in many cases, fathers completely abandon or neglect their responsibility to teach their sons how to be men. This results in men growing up as grown males, and not having the slightest clue as to what it means to be a man. It's up to you to break this chain, set goals and take action!

I have the privilege of talking to many female clients on a daily basis who express their desires to be in a relationship with a man. They feel as though they are submissive and would like to be lead by a man, but under no circumstances are they willing to submit to just *any* man. They want to submit to a man who is led by God, has submitted to God and is prepared to lead her into prosperity. To be quite honest, I don't follow anyone who doesn't have a solid plan and *I'm* a man.

My time is too valuable to waste on ambiguity and that's exactly how women feel.

Women have to sacrifice a lot to be in a relationship with a man, so you have to be prepared to accommodate her. "What do you mean women have to give up a lot". Well when she marries you, she has to give up her maiden name and take on yours, she carries your baby for nine months and hopes to get her figure back, she takes care of the household and nurtures the people in it, and that's just for starters. A woman who is willing to do all of these things wants to be assured that she won't have to do so uncomfortably. Could you imagine having to struggle and carry a baby for nine months, bring him/her into a world with no security, and be disciplined by a man with no discipline?

You have to show a woman that not only do you have a plan for your own life, but you also have a plan for the life you are trying to build *together*. So often we men get distracted from our goals simply because we see a beautiful woman with a nice body. Sure, it's fun in the beginning, but before long, she will look at you and say "What's next". Oh you've been there before fellas, everything is going well; you're getting food, sex and peace of mind and then she hits you with "What are we?" "Where are we going with this?" "Are we in a relationship?"

Women want to be led, they want a plan, and they want to look forward to something fresh, exciting and new. When you first meet her, she wants you to initiate the conversation, ask for her number and then set up a date. She wants *you* to call her, take the time to get to know her, and then *plan* an actual date. After the first date, she will want another, then another, then another, and after she's comfortable being around you, she will want even more from you. At this point, she doesn't just want to date, she's attracted to you, the days, weeks and months are going by and she's not getting any younger.

After all this time spent together, she adores you and is fascinated about what you're going to do next. She sees the value in you and is wondering if you see the value in her. She wants for you to ask her to be exclusive so that the two of you can grow together and build a legacy. She will have faith in you *today* if you show her that you have plans on remaining in her life *tomorrow*. When you don't take steps towards growth, you give a woman doubt about where the two of you stand in the relationship.

The vast majority of young women aspire to one day be in a loving marriage, have children, a nice house and all the wonderful things that come with it. She's looking for her knight in shining armor and she's hoping that that person is *you*. Yes, I know, marriage is the furthest thing from your mind right now because you're too focused on your next paycheck, and that's fine. By all means, get your personal and professional life together, but if you're investing time in a woman, know that she's expecting you to lead. If you can't afford to date, then don't!

Yes, there are many women who date for free meals, but we're going to focus this part of the discussion on the women of substance. Women of substance are tired of dating endlessly and aimlessly, tired of sleeping around and are looking for something solid/serious. All she wants is a man, who will love her, protect her, provide for her and do so on a consistent basis and be loyal. If none of those things are in your plans, then you are not ready to be in a relationship with a woman. The idea is to have a plan to constantly upgrade your relationship or marriage so that it doesn't get stale.

For example, if you're interested in a woman and she's your co-worker, associate from church or classmate, upgrade the relationship to a *friendship*. A friendship will allow you to build a closer and more genuine relationship with a woman without any added pressure. You will open up a side of her that is warm, loving and sincere, and you will show her that same side of you. During this time, you will begin to explore what one another values and can then figure out how you can add value to her life. If taking the time to build with a woman isn't a part of your plan, you are not ready to be in a relationship with a woman.

If you are willing to take your time and get to know her, you'll have the perfect opportunity to upgrade the friendship to dating. This is where the two of you get to not only talk about the things you like, but you get to experience them. Women love to be entertained and you can never go wrong with taking a woman out on a date. Most women are so deprived of a good date that she's likely to drop everything she's doing just to be out of the house with you. All she needs to know is the time, date, location and it's a date!

Why would a woman drop everything that she's doing just to go out on a date with a man? Because she wants companionship, she wants to be seen in the latest fashion, glammed up and on the arm of a great man. Sure, she can take herself out, sure she can go out with her girls, but that gets old and she wants something new. This is what makes you so valuable to a woman, you have the opportunity to show her a good time and become a go-to source for fun and excitement.

The more you plan to show a woman a good time, the more she will want to be around you. Consequently, if you neglect the planning process, she will eventually get bored with you and outsource for fun and excitement. The whole point of being in a relationship is to enjoy being *together*, so it's important to give her a reason to be in a relationship with you. It doesn't get any simpler than figuring out a time, date, location and activity and extending the invitation to your lady. Plainly put, she doesn't want to be the only one who has fresh ideas and the desire to enjoy life as a couple.

You will find that when you meet a woman's folks, one of the first questions they will ask is your plan for the future. Why do they care? They care because they're not getting any younger, they want the best for their daughter and they want to see their grandchildren grow up. You may be charming and good-looking, but none of that matters when it comes down to their daughter and her future. They want to know that you are ready, willing and able to protect and provide. And rightfully so; you wouldn't give your daughter away to some guy who didn't have a plan would you?

The key to a long-lasting relationship is planning for it to last. You have to think about tomorrow, next month, next year and years to come, not just right now! You have to be honest with yourself about where you are in life and what your plan is for your future. Having a plan for your own life should be a pre-requisite for planning a future with a woman. A woman will believe in you for as long as you show signs of moving forward, and once those signs dwindle, she's be moving out.

Enjoy the dating experience, the friendship and the previous association and then upgrade to a committed relationship. Upgrade your new relationship by introducing your partner to the people who are important in your life. Propose the idea of marriage and confess your love to her before God and witnesses. Fall deeper in love, have children and build your legacy. Once you've got the girl, treat her as if you're trying your best to keep her. Don't let the relationship get old, keep it fresh and new.

A Woman Doesn't Like To Share Her Man

One thing I've come to learn about women is when they love they love *hard*! Meaning they will do whatever it takes to keep their man happy and to make sure that he never leaves. With that being said, there's no room for any other woman to interfere with what she's worked so hard for. That goes for your mother, the mother of your child (if applicable), ex's and/or female friends. She is claiming you as her one and her only and will not tolerate anyone who poses a threat to the relationship.

Now, I know it sounds like she may be a little bit crazy, but there's nothing wrong with marking your territory and protecting it. When you have a good thing, many people will set out to come and take what you have. We've all witnessed at some point or another where a person's relationship status has changed, and then all of a sudden that person became more interesting. The only thing that became more interesting is that they are off limits and those who seek a challenge view that as a challenge. This same theory applies to women as well, some women don't value relationships and marriage and will try to come in and wreck your home.

The best way to avoid temptation is simply to avoid temptation. We all know the seductive power of a beautiful woman and what it does to a man. You're human, no one is expecting for you to not be attracted to a woman. What's expected of you is to not open up the door for her to walk in and seduce you. The only thing worst than cheating physically is cheating emotionally. You've seen in the movies where a man cheats on a wife, she finds out and then she asks, "Do you love her?"

She's curious as to whether or not you love her because your response will determine just how deep the relationship truly is. If you love her, then she'll feel as though the damage is irreconcilable, if you don't she'll believe there's still hope. Even if cheating never escalates to the physical, a woman will still be hurt simply by your hearts desire for another woman. The thought that you would initiate conversation, express your innermost thoughts and feelings to another woman is cheating. You're sharing your time, energy and emotions with another woman outside of your relationship.

This is where a lot of men constantly get it wrong. He'll say, "But babe, we didn't sleep together" and think that because there was no penetration that it's not cheating. Cheating is any welcomed or initiated interaction outside of your relationship with a woman you know is romantically interested in you. That lunch date that you went on that you know is not strictly business, or that text message after hours, or that Facebook friend request you accepted from your ex. All of those instances open up the door to foul play.

A woman wants to feel special, as if she's the only woman in your world. Of course you can't avoid interacting with other women, however you can control the level of interaction with them. Not everyone who is around your circle needs to be in your circle. In fact, if you wouldn't feel comfortable introducing her to your significant other or inviting her into your home amongst your family, she probably doesn't belong in your life. When it comes to business, communication should take place during business hours on your business email or phone or at the office. Women in the workplace don't need to have access to your personal life, that's where your partner comes in.

By setting the barriers, you give your lady a sense of security, which builds trust in the relationship. Consequently, when you allow other women to crossover into your personal space, you raise a red flag in your partner's mind because the other woman belongs in your *business* space. In her mind, she'll be thinking, "Woah! What is she doing here at his birthday party/family gathering/etc? Out of all the people he could invite, why would he invite *her*?" You may think that everything is all smiles, peaches & cream but from that moment on, she will never be ok with this woman's presence in your life.

Every time you mention or invite this particular woman to anything, she'll grow suspicious, and rightfully so. You must know where to draw the line with your associates, co-workers, friends and counterparts. You'll have to learn this with your guy friends, lady friends, family members and relatives as well. You're only one person, I know but you'll have to figure out a way to prioritize, and make your lady a #1 priority in your life. When you don't make her a priority, all kinds of problems can arise.

For starters, you're making her unhappy and that's no way to treat someone who is significant in your life. You have to remember that men and women value different things. Us men can go to work from 9am-5pm, grab drinks with the guys from 5pm-9pm, come home at 10pm looking for dinner and sex, and by 10:10pm (lol) want to be left alone so we can sleep. And to us, that sounds like heaven on earth, and we're ready to do it all over again until the end of time. Meanwhile, your lady is miserable because you're not taking her needs into consideration.

You've given your job your full-time, your boys your undivided attention, and come home to give the love of your life your drunken leftovers? That's because your priorities aren't in order and you're not taking care of home. In your mind, you're probably thinking, "Babe, I'm just hanging out with the guys after work", but in reality, you are cheating her out of your time with her. You aren't being fair about the level of investment you signed up to make. Instead you are having your cake and eating it too.

Just imagine being in a relationship where you are loving, supportive, and most importantly loyal, and take care of your household, meanwhile, your lady dresses up every night after work as if she's going on a hot date, but turns out to just be another "ladies night out". By the time she gets home, her feet hurt, she's tired, no dinner was cooked and to top it off she's in no mood for romance. She may very well be just hanging out with the girls, but that's not the point. The reality is that she's investing more time in her job and in her girls than she's giving to her man at home.

There's a way to avoid this division and that's by sticking together, knowing who's for you and who's simply with you for the time being. Sharing your time with the wrong individuals can land you with that person full-time. Hanging out with the guys doesn't sound so exciting anymore *now* does it? Even your boys know that they have to make time for their lady and can't afford to spend all of their time with you. There's nothing wrong with hanging out, just find balance.

Your boys however, are the least of your woman's worries. She's more concerned about the women you allow into your life. When you get into a relationship, your lady should be your one and only female friend. That girl that you've been knowing since childhood, yea give her a virtual kiss goodbye and save your kisses for your ladies. All of the women from your past need to stay in the past. If you have a child from a previous relationship, the two of you need only communicate with one another as it pertains to the child.

Remember, women care about the emotional attachment you have to other women and will grow suspicious if you have any type of "special connection". With your mother, it's expected for you to have an emotional connection. However as a man you should be strong enough to let go and cater to your lady as your father should cater to your mother. It shouldn't be a competition between the two and there is room for the both of you; just make sure to prioritize. Your mother needs to know that you have a woman in your life, and your woman needs to know that your mother is an important part of your life.

A woman wants a man who can offer her security and be there for her exclusively. It's not exclusive if you're sending her the same "Hello beautiful, how are you?" text. It's not exclusive if you're still dating and sleeping with other women. It's not exclusive if you aren't claiming her as your woman. And it's not exclusive if other women get to experience the same perks that she gets to experience.

If you're in a committed relationship, a woman shouldn't have to share you with another woman, you should be loyal. Offer her the security that she deserves and that you would want another man to offer your mother, sister, or daughter. There are so many reasons why sharing yourself in an adulterous way is wrong, but most importantly it dishonors you and your relationship. If you're unable to be faithful in a relationship, just stay single until you are ready. When you're finally ready to commitment, be ready to share your world only with the one you love.

Chapter 4:

Courtship

Friendship Is The Key To Romance

Good friends are hard to find, and that's exactly what makes friendship with a woman so special. Throughout your life you will encounter many different women who are amazing for all sorts of reasons, but your *friends* will be few. A friendship with a woman is sacred because of the intricate details that go into *why* you are connected in the first place. Before you can unlock the door to a woman's body, you must first unlock the door to her heart, and you'll achieve this through friendship.

Now, I know what you're thinking, "I'm not sitting in no woman's friend zone" and I'm with you on that. I assure you that you won't have to sit in a woman's friend zone, or waste your time giving your all to a woman who gives you nothing in return. What I'm about to reveal is one of the staples that are missing from many failed relationships. Often times we are so eager to pursue our physical connection instead of first focusing on a spiritual connection. Our goals are short-term which is why we as men often struggle with maintaining long-lasting relationships.

In order for you to be a great friend to someone, simply put, you have to have some sort of value. If a woman of substance sees value in you, she will likely want to associate with you on some level or another. If she sees no value in you, she won't entertain the thought of building any kind of relationship with you. By value, I don't simply mean monetarily because "spending power" attracts all women. By value I mean that there is something deep inside of you beyond the surface that makes its way above the surface and manifests itself to everyone around you.

When we hear the word *friendship* we sometimes think "platonic" and that's not where I'm going with this. When I say friendship, I mean that you are connected to a woman for reasons that pertain to the heart. It means that there is a mutual respect for one another and there is also the possibility for growth. When you are apart, you figure out more and more ways to come together. You see value in her thoughts; her time and her resources and the feelings are mutual.

A friendship is an out of body experience that will take your relationship to the next level. It is the foundation to a happy, healthy, longer-lasting relationship. Isn't it strange how after a break-up some like to say, "We will forever remain friends"? If the friendship were true from the beginning, the relationship would have no end. Claiming to somehow miraculously manage to be friends after a break-up is merely a sign that one or both parties can't let go. Real friends take the time to understand each other, and will do whatever is necessary to maintain the relationship. A break-up is a sign that the moral fibers that are found in a true friendship were never there.

Take a look around a construction site and the first thing you'll see is bunch of men laying down a foundation. Why are they doing this? They're doing this because they understand that the foundation is the key to the entire development. In years to come when you see that the building is still standing, there will be an even greater appreciation for the foundation that was laid down year's prior. It's an investment that needed to be made; skipping over this process would sabotage the entire development, as the building will have nothing left to stand on. Building on that particular spot at that particular time wasn't by accident, they had a plan that was carried out through a wide array of partnerships.

Your relationship is the equivalent of a building development and a friendship is the foundation. Until you take the time to dig below the surface and do the necessary work on the ground level, you'll stunt the growth of your relationship. By introducing the idea of friendship, you'll open up the door for valuable insight that will help you move forward and up with your partner. If you skip over this process, you may miss the opportunity to even get started on a development.

First, a woman wants to know that you can be trusted with information. This is a very simple test that any man can pass; simply make yourself available to her by listening and offering sound advice. Once a woman feels comfortable sharing information with you, she will constantly pour into you. Be genuine and sincere and she will *invite* you into her life. Show compassion and concern and you'll become a go-to source for her to express her innermost thoughts and feelings.

Then, a woman will want to know that you value her time. If you've made plans with a woman, be sure to be on time, and if you cannot make it, let her know in advance. Being considerate of a woman's time will keep you in a woman's favor and will gain her respect. Canceling on a woman or showing up late will have the opposite effect and will cause her to lose faith in you as a suitable friend. A true friend in a woman's eyes is always available, accessible and dependable.

In a friendship, a woman wants to know that you truly care about her as a person. Your attitude towards her will reveal everything she needs to know about the friendship. When it comes to a commitment, you should pursue a woman that you love and can tolerate. If you're her friend, a woman will look to you to do both. If you can't make it through a friendship, there's no way you'll last in a marriage.

Ultimately, that's what building a friendship is all about; building something that will last forever. Once you become married, there won't be any room for any other friendships with women, because remember, "Friendship is the key to romance". All the time you've invested building a friendship with your lady was in hopes that it would lead to romance. Now that you've got her, she is your one and only female friend. To avoid conflict in your relationship, leave all off the other woman who are looking to build a friendship with you on the outside looking in.

If you need a woman to listen to your problems, turn to your lady. If you need a woman to do you favors, turn to your lady. If you need a woman to escort you to an event, turn to your lady. If you're looking to go into business with a woman, turn to your lady. If you can't turn to your lady for any and all of the things listed above, chances are you've chosen the wrong lady.

Since friendship is the key to romance, you cannot to allow another friendship with a woman to transpire once you already have one. Women are territorial and rightfully so; they don't like the idea of sharing any aspect of their man with another woman. That includes your mind, body, time and resources; she wants you to remain exclusive with all of the above. The only person who should have access to these things is the woman whose earned it; the woman you're committed to. It's impossible to be loyal to two women at one time, and women are smart enough to know when another woman has her heart set on *more* than friendship from her man, because friendship was the route *she* took to get you.

A friendship is a test that a woman puts a man through before she rewards him with anything more. This gives her time to figure out who you are as a person, and how you'll fit into her life. She'll get close enough to see how attached you are to other women, the type of women who have your attention, and how emotionally available you are to receive her. Through getting to know you, you will reveal all she needs to know about your character, and whether or not she wants you to play a role in her life. In friendship, there is no commitment, however there is *loyalty*, which she will give you the opportunity to prove.

To be a true friend to a woman requires a great deal of loyalty, as it will demand your undivided attention. Women are notorious for paying close attention to detail, and they notice when you aren't noticing them. She will know when your mind is divided between her and another woman because your time, energy, effort and resources will be scarce. By focusing your energy on coming up with new ideas to enhance your friendship with a woman, you'll manage to stay relevant. Go the extra mile to add value to that friendship and you'll eliminate the competitors.

It's common for a man to pursue a woman for her body and overlook her mind, but that yields only a short-term victory. Use friendship as the foundation and you will tremendous value added to the quality of your relationship. With friendship comes *true* love, respect and honor and these things come over time. Take as much time as you need to develop the friendship, lay down the foundation and build on it. Friendship is the key to romance!

Be A Gentlemen

When we're hanging out with our boys, we're rough, tough, and insensitive and can often times be quite selfish. This type of behavior works amongst other men because over time we've developed the tough skin for it. We're used to closing off our emotions, not expressing our feelings, and sharing as little as possible with one another. Since childhood, our father tells us to stop crying when we cry, get back up as soon as we fall, and toughen up if we show any type of emotion. This type of behavior works well with other men, but will prove to be counter-productive when dealing with a woman.

Every lady is a woman, but not every woman is a lady. You can tell the difference simply by observing a woman's behavior patterns. A woman and a lady are both sensitive and emotional, however a lady will make a point to take better care. The reason for this is because she's been groomed physically, emotionally and psychological into knowing whom she is and what she's worth. Women who lack this home training are still trying to figure out their worth. With that said, a lady will have higher standards than the average women and will require more of you.

That's the beauty of being with a lady; she will motivate and inspire you to be a better man, and a gentleman. She will help you to bring out the sensitive and emotional side that you've been trying so hard to hide all of your life. She will show you that strong men *do* cry, they *do* hug/kiss, they *do* say I love you and they *do* show compassion. That's because a lady has *substance*, consisting of good morals, values and principles that she'll be willing to share with you. It's impossible for a woman to give out something she is without.

Choosing the right women to open your heart to is very important because you'll be sharing your values. That means everything you've built over the years will be accessible to them. Your family, friends, assets and network will all be within arms reach. Not everyone who is around your circle needs to be in your circle. A lady will be attracted to a gentleman, but a woman will be attracted to whatever looks and feels good at the moment.

A woman who hasn't been groomed to become a lady simply won't know any better, which in turn won't inspire you to *be* better. She'll accept you exactly as you are as opposed to helping you reach higher goals. She won't care if you have a sensitive or emotional side because as far as she knows, "that's just how men are". She doesn't understand her role as a woman, she doesn't understand that a man's sensitive and emotional side has been hidden and needs to be brought out, she doesn't understand a man because she hasn't taken the time to understand herself. She won't look to you to be a gentleman because she hasn't reserved the right to require one.

What does being with this type of woman mean for you as a man? It means that you will continue to speak to women in the same tone and in the same manner as you would another man. You will continue to be rough, tough and insensitive to women's feelings. You won't look to be romantic because you're in a relationship with a woman who doesn't have any standards or requirements, not because she doesn't secretly desire it, but because she doesn't have the confidence to require it. She's missing the *substance* that can be found only in the woman who has been seasoned and empowered by other men and women.

You will come across many women who lack confidence and esteem and your job as a man is to be gentle. Encourage her by letting her know that she is worthy, she has value and that she matters. Preying on the weak is a sign of weakness, instead set your goals higher and aspire to be with a woman who is strong. Your encouragement could inspire countless women to give more, become more and go after more. These are our daughters, sisters, mothers and caregivers so we must be gentle and protect them at all costs.

Being gentle doesn't have to apply to only women; you can start being gentler towards other men as well. Doing so will strengthen your relationship with other men because they'll feel more comfortable opening up to you about matters of the heart. This could improve your relationship with your son, brother, father and your friends. There is nothing wrong with expressing matters of the heart with another man; in fact communion is what being a man is all about. A closed heart is a closed mind.

My seven-year-old son Ethan is a blessing because he helps me to grow as a man. He shows me how to be patient, loving and kind and it has greatly improved the quality of my life. I use what he teaches me and I apply it when I'm speaking to his mother, my family, my friends and everyone around me. I give my son hugs and tell him that I love him on a regular basis because I want him to know that *this* is what a man of substance does. My son models himself after me so it's important that I instill in him the morals, values and principles that make a man great.

When I look at my son, first of all he looks *just* like me, so it takes me back to my childhood. My father passed when I was only one year old and I could count on both hands how many times my step-father hugged me and told me he loved me. That hurt me as a child and as adult, knowing that someone so close could emotionally be so distant. I want to make sure that my son never experiences that feeling, is showered with love, and understands the power of emotions. Tapping into your emotions will help you to grow as an individual, in your community and will inspire your life's work.

There's no way I could possibly write books on relationships without accessing my sensitive and emotional side. A relationship with anyone or anything is a very sensitive and emotional thing. Ignoring your emotions or shying away from them will only block your creativity and progress. It's common for people who are emotionally unavailable to block off their feelings, so when they finally give access to it, it's like a breath of fresh air. It takes time to come to this place, this calm of the spirit, but once you've reached it, everyone will know you have arrived.

Being a gentleman will inspire the way you walk, talk and carry yourself. You'll have discovered the value in your emotions and no longer see the value in hiding them. You'll have swallowed your pride, humbled yourself and now seek validation only from God. You will forget that you're from the streets, and start setting your eyes on the paths of the entire world. When you're in Rome, do as the Romans do.

When people see you, they'll see a tunnel of light as opposed to a dark cloud in the sky. Not only will you have brought peace into your own heart/mind, you will inspire others to do the same. They'll wonder "What made him shave and throw on a suit" or "What made him start bringing his family to church" or "What made him decide to send all of the staff greeting cards and give holiday bonuses *this* year". You will attract positive attention because a positive perspective has been implemented in your life. The world is dark enough, cold enough and hard enough already; your gentle touch will stand out every time.

A gentle approach will open up countless doors in business, in love and in life. A company loves it when you follow instructions on an application process, or have done your research and are passionate about the job you are seeking. It shows that you have love inside of you and that you'd be willing to put love into the work you'll be doing for their company. You'll increase company moral with your kind heart, great attitude and loving spirit. You'll be sensitive to the thoughts and feelings of your fellow co-workers and subordinates and that attitude will move you far up in the ranks.

A lady loves it when a man is gentle because for them, being gentle is a standard. They require that you take care of them, protect them and provide for them because this is something that a lady does for herself. If you want to increase your chances of attracting a lady, it will simply require you to be sensitive to her needs. That means you will have to tap into your emotional, sensitive and gentle side to prepare yourself. That doesn't mean you have to lose your edge, but simply create a space in your heart that is reserved just for her.

In life in general, people will respect you more when you are considerate of them and their situation. After all, it's the human thing to do, and anything less would be uncivilized. Acts of kindness doesn't come only from saints; it comes from regular everyday people like you and me. Help those you see are in need simply because it needs to be done; this is what you would want others to do for you. Be the man who is known for acts of kindness, so that you may inspire change in the hearts and minds of others. If you want to lead, give people something worthy of following.

Take Your Lady Out

Us men can be very simple; all we want is food, sex and peace of mind. The world is cold and hard towards men, so when we get home, we just want to cater to ourselves or be catered to. We enjoy doing absolutely nothing until it's time to do something. We can literally go to work, come home to eat, watch TV, have sex and go to sleep every day for the rest of our lives with absolutely no complaints. Sounds like a great life doesn't it? There's only one problem, you forget about your lady!

Women and children have a lot in common, so when you're in a relationship, try to imagine yourself taking care of a child. A child won't want to stay in the house all day, they want to go outside to see the world and the wonderful people in it. And they won't just want to go to the same old park; they'll want to try new things like Disney land, the zoo, a museum or aquarium. They get bored very easily and look to their provider for entertainment and excitement. Neglect a child who is seeking your attention and it will only be a matter of time before they seek and find attention elsewhere.

Women are the same way; they don't want to be in the house watching TV, feeding you and having sex all day and every day. They want to go out and explore the world and the wonderful people in it. They want to go and see latest movie, the most popular Broadway show, or travel to a different part of the world. They want to go out and do things and not just sit idle in the house. Being a couch potato might be fun for you, and might initially be fun for her, but over time she will want *more* from you.

Being in a relationship is an investment, and the return you will gain from catering to your lady will prove to be priceless if done properly. The first step to a good investment is to spend your time getting to know someone that you genuinely care about. Dating will feel like a burden to you if you aren't in love with the person you're on the date with. You'll start to count every minute and every penny because you don't feel you're getting back what you feel your time and money is worth. Investing in a woman you love will not only change your attitude towards your time and money, but also towards *her*.

If you don't see a woman in your future, chances are she doesn't belong in your life right now. Your time is too valuable to spend it on a woman who isn't adding value to your life. So spare yourself the wasted time, energy, effort and money and invest more into yourself until you've found the one. This will give you time to date yourself which will require you to spend time and money. You'll gain a new appreciation for the art of dating when you understand the *cost* associated with it.

If you factor in the cost for you alone to travel, have one drink and have one meal, and then include the time associated, you can double that when incorporating a woman. A woman will look to you to be the provider, that means paying for everything. Don't feel bad, men are simple remember? In exchange, we get to have our *simple* desires fulfilled in the long run. A date is simply an opportunity to entertain the lady you are in a relationship with or at least see as potential. This is your opportunity to show your leadership skills, passion and creativity.

One thing I love about women of substance is their creative minds; they always look to do more, see more and have more. As a man, that motivates me and inspires me to work harder to meet that standard. For men, everything is black and white, cut and dry, but with women of substance there is color and/or a gray area. A woman of substance will get you off of the couch, out into the world going to new places, meeting new people and doing new things. It's healthy to be in a relationship that inspires constant growth and movement into more promising directions.

People grow apart in relationships in part because there's no passion, there's no excitement and quite frankly they're bored! In the beginning of the relationship, there was great conversation, date nights, traveling, etc. Now that you've got the girl, all of those things slowly but surely disappeared. A lady doesn't require much when it comes to dating; all she really requires is *consistency*. Understanding what a woman of substance requires of a man will help you to prepare your investment portfolio psychologically, emotionally and financially.

It might save you time, energy, effort and money to never go anywhere or do anything, but that doesn't do much for your lady. Now there's nothing wrong with just having movie night at home, cooking dinner or just hanging out, but their needs to be some time of balance. Otherwise, she'll end up finding something to do without you, or worst she'll find something to do with another man. And that's the part you need to realize; women love the idea of companionship and will acquire it at any costs. If you wont invest the time, energy, effort and money, there's always a man patiently waiting around who will. These men are commonly known as "male friends"; their role is to be there for your lady especially during those times when there's trouble at home.

The key then is to keep your lady entertained. Use your leadership skills and creativity to figure out a way to make it last forever. Not only will you feel better about yourself as a man for being able to sustain your position, but your lady will respect you all the more for trying. Most men who are on the outside looking in will try their best to figure out a way into your woman's life, and entertainment will be amongst their first proposals. If the men on the outside can understand this about your woman, then you should be an expert at understanding your woman because you're the one who's with her.

And don't think that because a woman doesn't speak up that she doesn't want to go anywhere or do anything, she's not speaking up because she's probably already checked out. She no longer looks at you as her source of entertainment as has found a better way to enjoy life. This can all be avoided simply by paying attention to her needs and catering to them. Taking your lady out has to be a regular thing; it doesn't have to be every night, but it should certainly happen at least once out of the week.

On Sunday, you can take her to church and then afterwards, grab some ice cream and go for a walk in the park and talk about the things that are important to you both. When you have a woman of substance, it's not always about the dollar being spent, but rather the time that's being invested. She's aware that men value both their time and their money, so she's paying close attention to how willing you are to invest both. What matters most to her is your attitude towards her when it comes to spending time together. She wants to have a close relationship and constantly looking for new ways to improve it *together*.

On Monday, you can surprise her at work; convince her to take a quick lunch break so that you can have a quick chat. Prepare a special home cooked meal that she loves and share it with her. Find a spot in the lobby for all of her co-workers to see or a bench outside where you both can get some fresh air. It's a very small gesture but it would mean the world to your lady because it shows that you care enough about her to *make* time for her. A woman loves it when her man is always busy taking care of his business, but never too busy for her.

You're only out of options once you've stopped thinking. And when you care about the happiness of your significant other, you never stop thinking of ways to improve the quality of your relationship. Women of substance respect leadership, and will follow you anyplace that motivates and inspires her to be in a relationship with you. It doesn't have to be any place fancy, all she wants is for you to focus your energy on figuring out a way to make her feel special. The thought alone is enough to give her hope and that's all she's asking for.

The best part about taking your lady out on a date is she will want to somehow return the favor. She appreciates the time, energy, effort and money you've invested in her and she will want to give you a return on your investment. You want to keep your lady interested, and the best way to do that is by showing interest in her. You give a little to get a little. At the end of the day, both parties are happy, satisfied and optimistic about tomorrow.

If you choose the right woman, she will make the best of your time, help you grow your money and give you peace of mind. Challenge yourself to be creative, compassionate, and most of all interested in your lady's special requests. Investing in her will give you great pleasure because she has proven herself worthy and is a valuable asset to your life. It pays to keep the person who brings you happiness satisfied, and is a worthy investment hands down. Take pride in the relationship you have, never grow complacent, and constantly find new ways to keep your lady entertained.

Know Your Worth

We always warn women about the dangers that come with dealing with men, don't we? We sit them down, talk them death, and even try to segregate them from the male population as if men are some sort of plague. The reality though is that danger can come from any gender, any angle, and any relationship. The brothers are often overlooked when it comes to these forewarnings because society expects us to simply know how to protect ourselves or worse, bounce back after we get used, abused and mistreated. Today, I'm here to tell you that just as sure as a woman should know her worth you too should know yours.

As men, there are two things that we value the most and that is our money and our time. After all, we work hard to get the things we have and we shouldn't have to fork it over to anyone who hasn't earned it. There are plenty of charities out there that we could donate to if we're feeling generous. You have a busy schedule and it's hard enough simply being a man and surviving, let alone investing time and money into a woman. For this reason, you should place high value on your time and money.

As you continue to expand your network, you will meet many beautiful and successful women. Some of which equate their success in their career to *value* in a relationship. They've got their college degree(s), nice car, house, great career and the list goes on an on. They treat themselves to fine dining, trips around the world, they've got friends who are well-known public figures and they consider themselves "high class". Yes, I know what you're thinking, "How do any of the things listed benefit *me*?"

I'm glad you asked! As quality men of substance and as leaders, we don't look for a woman to provide for us, chauffer us, or connect us. As men, we take pride in providing for our family and ourselves, getting behind our *own* wheels, and making the connections. Doing these things makes us feel better as a man, so meeting a woman who wants to do it for us isn't our type of woman anyway. However, there are many women who feel as if her material things have value to a man and will try to use it as leverage.

I remember meeting a woman online who was a very popular in the modeling industry, she was gorgeous, had a body to die for and clearly was highly sought after. None of those things mattered to me, I simply was interested in meeting and interacting with her to see if she had any substance. We would talk and I would ask questions that would require her to give substantial answers that would help me draw certain conclusions before our first date. As a relationship expert, I do come across women who are interested in mental stimulation and nothing further. To a woman, they call that a friendship, to me I call that a *client*.

While talking to her, she would speak of another guy she was dating which was a red flag that she wasn't interested in *me*, but I played along. I would listen to her relationship problems and give very vague answers like "Oh my" or "I see". After all, she hasn't hired me to be her personal relationship coach, so what made her think I was interested in listening to her relationship problems? I continued to listen because sometimes that's all a person needs, and she was content with that. We made a little bit of progress as I was able to conclude that her heart was someplace else.

Prior to us meeting, she made it clear that us getting together wasn't a date, and I obliged. Right then, and there when she made it clear that it was not a date, that's when the terms changed. Now, we're simply two friends meeting, chatting and enjoying each other's company. As friends, we mutually respect one another's time, energy, effort and money and neither party has expectations of the other. Normally when I got out with my friends, it's understood that we are all adults here and we are responsible for our own bill.

Not all women, but some women feel they are *entitled* to have men pay their bills, treat them to dinners, and provide for them. Boy did she get a wake up call that day. When I think of a first date or a meet and greet, I'm thinking a coffee shop, walk in the park, or someplace where we can focus on one another and talk briefly. In this case, I had forgotten that I was dealing with a woman who felt she was entitled to royal treatment. I made the mistake of letting her choose the place to go and it cost me more than I would have liked to invest in a woman who had no interest in me.

We went far out to a nice Sushi spot where we sat and dined. I ordered maybe 6 pieces of sushi because I only ate sushi for taste, I didn't eat sushi to get full. Meanwhile, she ordered maybe 20 pieces of sushi, kinds that she never even tried before simply because she thought it was going to be all on me. I asked her "Are you going to eat all of that" and she replied "Oh I'm going to take some home with me". Now this is our first time meeting, so I felt insulted that she would so recklessly order everything on the menu. After all, that's not something that friends who respect each other would do.

I knew right then and there that if this is what she expected from me every time we went out, that this would be the very last time we went out. I don't mind investing in a woman, but when there's no return on the investment, it's just spending. I had no interested in spending on her or any woman for that matter, and I needed to send a clear message right away. I paid the bill, plus tip (around $80). It wasn't about the dollar amount it was about the principle. That $80 could've been better spent on a woman who deserved it and was genuinely interested in me.

After leaving the sushi spot, she requested that we go someplace else, and I thought to myself "Oh no! You're too expensive". In her mind, this was her opportunity to get treated and entertained on my bill. She thought that she was doing me a favor simply by being pretty and showing up. In my world, these types of women come a dime a dozen. We decided to stop at a bar for a drink; I figured it couldn't get too expensive *there*. She ordered up again, and I sat back in delight just watching her.

I would smile, drink, clink our glasses together with a "Just two friends hanging out" look on my face. The bill came to about $60, and to teach her a lesson about respect for her peers, I said, "So this rounds on you?"

and she replied "No". I asked "Why not?" and she said, "Because I don't want to". I then said "Well if we're going to be friends, we need to pay our own bills like friends do. And since I just paid the last bill which came up to $80, you can cover this one". She obliged, but was so bitter that a man stood up to her usury that she decided she no longer wanted to be friends.

She was gorgeous, fun to talk to and she had her own money; in fact I saw hundred dollars bills just lying around her car as we departed. It didn't bother me that she no longer wanted to be friends because she didn't treat me like a friend. No matter how beautiful or popular she was, that didn't add any value to my life. If a person doesn't add value to your life, they need to be subtracted from your life. She was used to walking all over men, and getting whatever she wanted from them, and I wouldn't allow her to do it to me. For that reason, I think she felt I wasn't her type, and I whole-heartedly agree.

You should never be the type of man a woman can take advantage of unless she is willing to reciprocate. You should never feel obligated to use your time, money and resources to accommodate a woman who has nothing invested in you. You should never equate outer beauty to inner beauty and confuse it with substance. You should never have to compromise your beliefs out of fear that a woman will abandon you. You should stand firm, know your value, know your worth and partner with a woman who has proven herself worthy.

On any given first date, $80 is way too much money to invest. A first date is about dialogue, getting to know the person and seeing if there's enough interest to pursue a second date. A brief 30 minute meet and greet at a coffee shop will suffice. If there's no interest on the first date, all you've lost was 30 minutes of your time and a few dollars on a coffee and muffin. If the date *did* go well, there will be plenty of opportunities to invest more on a second date. By now, you know she's worth it and you don't mind putting forth more effort.

There's nothing wrong with a man having standards and setting requirements for a woman. In fact, that should be your protocol when it comes to dating and relationships. Bringing something to the table will determine whether or not she gets to remain at the table, so pay attention to the value she's adding. The same way a woman can require you to do certain things to win her time, you can do the same. Women respect men who know their value and are bold enough to stand for what they believe in. If you don't know what your value is, take some time away from dating and relationships to figure it out.

Show Your Worth

One of the greatest investments you'll ever make in life is getting to know yourself. It's a long process, but it's worth it because you'll discover who you are, what you are capable of and how you can add value to the lives of others. Throughout the course of your life you will encounter people who will only associate with you based on what you can do for them. There's nothing wrong with that, it's simply a part of life. The key then is to find the greatness inside of you and let it *shine* so that others may grow dependent on your light.

When I was in middle school, I struggled with figuring out how to get the girls that I liked to come to me, but my older brothers were experts at it. I had a lot of guy friends, and these friendships were developed simply by me being myself. I wouldn't stutter when I talked to my boys, nor would I blush or act shy/timid when they came into the room, so why was I acting this way with the girls? The issue was that I was placing more value in them than I placed in myself. My boys acknowledged my skills as an athlete, singer, person, etc. but that was because I commanded it.

I soon figured out that I could also command respect from women simply by being myself. I liked the thought of that because now I didn't have to exhaust myself stepping outside of my comfort zone to prove that I'm worthy. All I had to do was carry myself as if I know that I'm worthy, but stay humble enough to acknowledge her worth. This was a #WinWin because everyone walks away feeling good about themselves.

Even better, we walk away *together* feeling good about ourselves.

The girls thought I was attractive, but I knew that looks could only get me so far. I would test my intellectual skills by writing them a love letter. Girls like it when you are able to stimulate their minds, and keep their attention. You'll gain even more points if you don't misspell any of the words. A woman wants a man who is good-looking, smart, romantic *and* resourceful. The more you showcase your abilities, the better your chances are at winning her over.

Any man can talk about how good he can treat a woman, or how much he is going to do for her, but a woman wants proof. She doesn't mind buying into your dreams, but before long, she will want to see the evidence. It's good to have dreams, and it's good to have goals, but if you don't have the means to provide what you're promising, you're only biding time. All it takes is a snap of a finger or a dial of a number and a woman can have another man replace you. Don't think for one second that you're her only option and that she *has to* settle for you, no she's giving you an opportunity to show her you are worth the wait.

It's no different from a woman asking you to wait until marriage; you see with marriage there's a deadline and you're in full control. All you have to do is propose, set the wedding date, get married and she's all yours. On the night of the honeymoon, it will be *her* turn to show and prove. Yes, it's time to see what all the fuss was about, and why you had to wait so long to cash in your rewards. And she will gladly show you.

But before we get to the honeymoon, you've got to get her attention, keep her attention and give her something to look forward to. Of all the billions of men in the world, why should she be bothered with *you*? This question should be like taking candy from a baby. You get to create a blueprint that the two of you can build upon, and lead the relationship wherever you want it to go. It's not as if she's inquiring because she wants you to fail, she's asking because she wants to know your plans for succeeding.

If you want a woman to stay, give her hope. If you want a woman to leave, give her doubt. Showing a woman your worth has more to do with you as a man, than it does with her as a woman. Granted, she does have to be emotionally available to receive you, however you can still show her that you can be of great value to her. You want to create an image and brand yourself as a quality man of substance so that when people in general think of you, they make *that* association. Once you place value on yourself, there won't be any confusion or argument about what you are worth, the world has to either take it or leave it.

When I was 27, I took a spiritual journey, and found myself living in a homeless. I knew I was worth *something*, but I hadn't yet figured out how much. While living in the shelter people would call on me for favors not knowing that I was going through a tough time in my life. At the time I thought that *I* was the one who needed the help, but I soon realized that I was being called to *be* the help. I didn't have money, a house, a car, all I had was *me*, my skills, my resources and my network.

I had a lot of time on my hands, so in the mornings I would go to Barnes & Nobles to read books on psychology, self-help, and marketing so that I could enhance my skills and put them on my resume. I had a Bachelor's degree and still no luck getting hired; I would apply to 100 jobs a day and still nothing. One day, I decided to submit my resume with a list of skills that I already had and recently acquired and filled out a volunteer application. Once the non-profit that I applied to read the skills and experience I had, they didn't want me as a volunteer, they wanted to hire me full-time.

Getting this new position helped me to see the value in everything I already had, and also helped me to go after more and always strive to better myself. What I learned from this experience is that the more you value you, the more the *right* people will want to partner with you. Not everyone will see value in you, but it's up to *you* to see value in yourself and show exactly what that value is. People are more willing to subscribe to someone who they feel will be a valuable asset to their lives. It does them no good to partner with someone who is going to be a liability.

You won't always have the opportunity to do the work and prove yourself, but you can always show up with a great attitude. In fact, your attitude will be the determining factor when it comes to your progress with a woman of substance. Women of substance more than likely will have their own money, car, house, career, degrees, etc so showing off yours won't have any effect on them. What will impress a woman more is your attitude towards your degree, how are you using it to help others? If you have a nice car and house, she'll want to know how many charities are you involved in?

Showing your worth means to show that you are worth the long-term investment. Assure her that going on a date, getting into a relationship, getting married or going into business with you isn't going to be a waste of her time. If you're going into it for anything short of love, you can rest assured that it won't last very long. Furthermore, you don't waste to waste *your* time on something that you know you aren't genuinely interested in. Instead, make wise decisions and put your best foot forward in hopes that a qualified candidate will take future steps with you.

While you're waiting, you should be working, and building yourself up. Women find men who have goals to be very attractive because it motivates them to do the same. All you have to do is be yourself, and present yourself as your best; do this and the right woman will love you for it. Go to school, get your education, establish your career and stay out of trouble. Strengthen your spiritual relationship with God, serve others, and surround yourself with positive people. Never look for a relationship, but always prepare your heart, mind, body and spirit to be ready for one.

A woman has to be in the right place spiritually and emotionally so hopefully she will be working on herself just the same. She will have experienced the good, the bad and the ugly and will now want an upgrade. She wants substance and by now, that's exactly what you're prepared to give her. She wants a man who takes care of his body, is educated, career oriented, driven and is open to love. Fortunately for you, that's exactly what you've been working on, and she can see it in you, which is why she'll be open to you.

Being true to self doesn't require a sales pitch or a gimmick; all you have to do is be yourself. You need to first do a soul search, and figure out what's missing from your life so that you can discover whom and what belongs in your life. The world won't know what you are capable of until you show them. A woman won't believe in you unless you give her something to believe in. Give her a reason to be with you, and she won't want to live her life without you.

Be Creative

Women love to experience *new* things; their minds are filled with imagination, and they love the idea of having an adventure. Sure, they could do it all by themselves or with their girls, but come on, she wants to spend time with *you*. The more creative you are with your adventures, the more she will look forward to experiencing them with you. The idea of you making plans, setting aside time and using your resources to make something happen will be all you need to brighten her day. Women get tired of the same old same old so switch it up every now and again.

One of the most common complaints that women have with men as that we are too simple, boring or that chivalry is dead. Now fellas, I'm the first to admit that I just want to chill and relax 7 days a week, 365 days a year. But with a seven-year-old child, that's simply not possible. When there's snow, he wants to build a snowman, make snow angels, or have a snowball fight. To him, it means the world, so of course I'm going to do it; it doesn't cost me anything but time, and it makes him happy, so in the end it's all worth it.

Guess what? Your lady would enjoy that experience in the snow just as much! Go ahead and ask her to join you outside, help you make a snowman, and make snow angels. Bring your camera, take fun pictures, and in the end have a fun snowball fight. It doesn't end there, when you get inside, you'll both be freezing, which is just in time for a hot cup of cocoa while watching a movie and relaxing. What started out as a spontaneous adventure in the snow has now ending in the warm arms of your lady. #WinWin

Sometimes that's exactly what it takes to keep the fire going in your relationship. All you have to do is come up with an idea that will put a smile on your lady's face and keep it there. If you've got a video recorder, video tape the moments, creative a nice video with pictures, music and sound, and give it to her as a birthday or Christmas gift. This thoughtful gesture will prove to be more valuable to her than any store bought item simply because of the love that went into creating it. By being creative, you are showing her that you feel she is worth putting forth time, energy and effort in addition to money.

Above anything else, a woman of substance admires a man with brainpower. She's not impressed with how much money you have or any other material thing, what matters to her is your willingness to continue making her happy. In order for you to keep a woman happy, you have to consistently be able to provide entertainment. That's all a woman wants is to be loved, protected, provided for and entertained on a consistent basis. If you can manage to focus on those four things, you will never run out of ways to keep her attention.

Being in a relationship is a job, and just like any other job, you can risk your position at the company by failing to deliver. Women get bored very easily and won't hesitate to seek entertainment elsewhere. To avoid this from happening to you, make yourself indispensable by being a go-to source for entertainment. That by no means insists that you should go broke trying to keep a woman's attention. In fact, we're not even talking about random women here; we're talking about *your* woman or someone you see as potential.

You're in full control and can take this in whichever direction you want to, your lady will follow your lead. Being creative doesn't have to involve a lot of money and it doesn't have to require a lot of time, all you really need is a lot of love. Find something that you're passionate about or something that she's passionate about and make an evening of it. I love to eat, and I also love to cook, and this makes for a great way to spark up good conversation, showcase my culinary skills, and also teach her a thing or two. Not to mention, enjoying a delicious meal together afterwards.

Playing basketball is also something I love to do, so for me, taking my lady out on the court, teaching her the game is a way that I can show her that I'm interested in spending quality time together. We would pack a couple of water bottles, some fruit, snacks and a sandwich and spend a day outdoors together. I'm sure if you left it up to your lady, playing basketball with you would probably be the last thing on her mind, but it's up to you as the man to take the lead, be creative and show her a good time. Plainly put, if you don't figure out a way to be creative, you will soon find yourself broke, alone or miserable. There's no real value in being with a woman who only wants you for your money, nor is there any real value in being with a woman who doesn't inspire you to do creative things for her.

You'll know you're in love with a woman when you're willing to do whatever it takes to make her happy. A red flag that she's not the one is when you view doing nice things for her as a chore. Of *course* you won't access the creative side of your brain if you yourself feels she isn't worth it. If she's not worth giving your best, than you're wasting each other's time. If she *is* worth it, prove it by tapping into your creative side and reminding her of why she chose you.

Just imagine meeting a woman who was the most amazing woman you've ever encountered. She gives great hugs, great kisses, great conversation, cooks great meals, and she's great everywhere else imaginable. She's constantly inviting you to holiday parties, family gatherings, fun outings, or nights in and every experience is awesome! You've never had a woman like this before and you're happy to have her in your life, and then all of a sudden, it all stops. There's no more invitations, no more special dinners, no more fun because she figured "I've got him now, no use wasting my time being creative anymore".

Or worst, imagine if she stopped doing all of those wonderful things you liked behind closed doors. See *now*, Houston we have a problem. Well that's how women feel about the fun and excitement going out of the relationship. They simply want to know that you still view them as your best friend and are interested in sharing your world with them. In fact, let this be a tool that you continue to use throughout the duration of your relationship. You can fix any aspect of your broken relationship with a little bit of creativity.

Once you stop being creative, a woman will start to feel neglected and underappreciated. Sometimes when we get set in a routine, we forget to *forget* about the routine and simply enjoy life. We neglect our partners because we sometimes get so caught up in our own personal interests that we forget that we're in this *together*. So now, you can't do the usual movie nights *at home* because you're trying to finalize some things for work. You have to take a rain check on making her favorite dish for dinner because you didn't take the time to get the ingredients from the grocery store.

Being creative requires you to *keep in mind* the people who are important and significant to you. When you pick up a candy bar from the newsstand, pick up one for your lady just to show her that you were thinking about her. Grab a rose or flower from a bush while you're on your way home and present it to her. When she opens the door, grab her and tell her lets go for a walk, talk about each other's day. It doesn't matter to her where you're going; at least she has something to follow.

Women LOVE spontaneity! Even if it's something as simple as taking a plain old board of checkers and playing games outside on the steps, she'll be up for it. She's intrigued by your availability and your willingness to invest your time. It's not about the game of checkers, or the snowman, or the walk around the neighborhood, it's about the *bonding* opportunity. Always keep in mind that a woman is fully capable of creating excitement for herself; when in a relationship though, she looks forward to having that experience with you.

If you have the power, the money or the resources to be extravagant, by all means use it to express your thoughts and feelings towards your lady. There's nothing wrong with splurging on the woman you love, just as long as it's done out of love. Any man can buy an expensive gift, but no man can creatively think like you. Every gesture you make should emphasize your love for your lady and place an even deeper imprint on her heart. When she speaks of you, she'll share her fondest members of the joy you bring, not just the gifts.

The idea here is to leave an emotional impression and make a spiritual connection that will last a lifetime. If it's her birthday, send her a rose for each age, and make a tradition of it. For Christmas, surprise her with one or more of the many things she's been talking about all year long. For New Years, create a photo collage or a video display showcasing memories from the previous year. On Mother's Day, make it a rule that she doesn't lift a finger until midnight. On everyday, create new ways to love one another.

Chapter 5:

Commitment

The Power Of Monogamy

Let me start off simply by saying that there are billions of women in the world, and you only need one. No matter where you go, you will always find extraordinary women who will blow your mind and the fact is, you simply can't have them all. There will be tall women, short women, big women, small women, and women whose curves are so unbelievable you can't even describe. While it may be fun to chase as many women as your heart desires at the beginning stages of your life, it will prove to add very little value to your life as you get older and start walking in your purpose. Don't feel bad, it's perfectly normal for a man to explore and see what's out there in the world, this is why they call getting married "settling down".

Not to mention, the more successful you become as a man, the more women will want to associate with you. And not just any women, but the one's you've always dreamed of. You know, coke bottle shape, gorgeous face, great in bed, don't talk much and on top of that is a "magician" and knows when to disappear. The one's that don't ask questions, will go along with anything, and won't require much. The reason why these women should remain in your dreams is because they won't add value to your life in reality. They will take you further and further away from being the quality man of substance you are destined to be and from walking in your purpose.

Once you grow up and mature, you will look back to those same women who didn't have any requirements, or standards, and were down for whatever and say, "I need more". When you reach a higher level of maturity, your values will shift and you will begin to go after what you *need* as opposed to what you want. This state of mind will humble you and give you a greater appreciation not only for yourself, but for other women. Learning to value and respect women is the key that will unlock the door to more positive relationships with other women, which will eventually lead to your happiness in a healthy relationship. This process doesn't happen overnight, it will take you some time to experience the bad before you appreciate the good.

After ripping and running from your mid teens into your late 20s and lord forbid your 30s+, the world around you will start to look at your life and will want to see progress/results. How does your personal decisions in relationships effect other people's association with you? I'm glad you asked. :) Your relationship choices shows your level of discipline, commitment, loyalty and devotion or the lack thereof. We all reserve the right to be selective when it comes to our relationships, however the choices we make will heavily influence how closely people on the outside looking in will choose to associate with us. People want to know that you are committed to something, whether it be getting back into shape, saving money, charitable giving, community service, raising a child, marriage or whatever.

The beauty in committing to someone or something in your life is the value the comes from it. When you commit to something, not only are you showing the recipient that you value the relationship, but you will inevitably be on the receiving end that comes with that union. Loyalty may be a small word, but it's a BIG thing. Maturity and growth is a part of growing up and it's essential to your success in life. You might have a favorite shirt that you liked, that perhaps over time you simply grew out of, and when you grew out of it you were forced to go out and look for something better. Had you held onto that shirt, not only will it have begun to deteriorate, but the people around you will also see your fear and/or reluctance to upgrade.

When it comes to relationships, women who are seriously looking to commit want to make sure that they are partnering up with the best. She wants the security of knowing that you are capable of taking care of yourself and have the heart to take care of her. The first thing she'll notice is the way you dress and carry yourself. This information should give you a heads up on how to prepare yourself for a relationship with other people. It's time to let go of the old, and upgrade to the new. That means a new attitude, new perspective, new heart, mind and spirit.

For so long, we've been cheating ourselves and spreading ourselves thin thinking that the best thing that could ever happen to us is getting fast and easy benefits from a woman. Getting benefits from a woman that you didn't earn only yields short term success. It's only a matter of time before either you get bored, or she requires more. Hopping from one woman to the next not only wastes your energy and money, but it also wastes valuable time that you can never get back, and it effects your credibility as a quality man of substance.

The same way us men don't want a woman who's been around the block and back is the same way women feel. There's no pride in knowing that the women you work with, went to school with, or for heaven's sake went to church with have all had a turn with you. It's just as shameful for a woman who's dating a man whore as it is for you dating a woman with a promiscuous past. A man should take pride in saving himself for marriage just as a woman should, and protect him name, reputation, and credibility at all costs. After all, this is the name that you eventually plan to share with a woman, and no woman wants to take on a name that's tainted.

But never mind the marriage for a second, as a man it's important that you have respect amongst your peers. If you don't have respect amongst your peers, then they certainly won't have respect for your marriage. Marriage is a full-time job, so before stepping into it, take on the job of being single, building up a positive name for yourself, getting your life in order, and preparing for the obstacles that will come when inviting a woman into your life. A marriage is a partnership, however you first have to become a suitable partner. Being in a marriage will be so much more enjoyable when you know your value and are able to consistently contribute your share to the union.

One of the most popular reasons for divorce is sheer boredom, followed swiftly by finances. While single, you have the opportunity to work on both having your finances in order and developing a tolerance for other people's thoughts and feelings. Committing to something for life is not something that you're being forced to do, so if you choose to go through with marriage, have a plan! If you don't plan for your marriage to succeed, then your marriage will eventually fail. If you plan accordingly, marriage will add tremendous value to your life and will continue to add value until death.

Many people bail out on marriage because it's not what they thought it would be. When many people think of marriage, they foolishly believe that there won't be any struggles, and that is far from the truth. In a marriage, you will experience *new* problems. Problems that didn't apply to a sex-driven relationship, where both parties were simply looking to have a good time. No, you see *now* there are *real* issues, *real* responsibilities, and *real* crisis that demand your attention. You will say to yourself "This is all new to me" on many occasions, just know that your wife will be saying the same thing. This is all new to you both because you have upgraded your relationship and are transitioning into new things.

What a married couple has that a regular boyfriend/girlfriend relationship doesn't is the *promise* that no matter what, they will stick together through the good, the bad and the ugly. That's the power of monogamy, you've got somebody who's got you. You ever look on an application where it asks you your "relationship status"? It never asks about the girlfriend because the word "girlfriend" in and of itself is enough evidence to show that the relationship has not yet grown to it's full maturity, so it is too soon to even acknowledge. A marriage on the other hand indicates that you have declared before the courts, God and witnesses that you have chosen to be with this person and vice versa for life.

There's a sense of pride in being able to declare your love, loyalty and commitment to someone before the courts, God and witnesses. You've just done something with your life that will forever be a part of your legacy. You've made a name for yourself, worked hard to become a quality man of substance, and then finally you've shared this honor with someone else. That's more than you can say for your past relationships, but *this* time, you're committed forever. Part of the reason your past relationships didn't last was because you never planned for them to.

Most of your past relationships were based on everything except the most important thing of all, love! If love isn't the foundation in your relationship, everything that you build on top of it will eventually crumble because it wasn't solid enough to hold it together. Yes, marriage is forever, but there's nothing to fear if you've chosen the best partner to enjoy the rest of your life with. You don't lose your independence when you exchange the rings, you gain something new called "Interdependence". That means that you no longer have to do everything all by yourself, you can depend on each other.

Let me break it down a little further for the brothers who are still on the fence about this "Declaration Of Interdependence". When you get married, hopefully you will have reached a level of maturity where you are 100% done with flirting, dating and sleeping with multiple women. More importantly, it is my great hope that you have finally found a woman who is not perfect, but is perfect for you. She accepts you for who you are, and is dedicated to helping you become even better than the way she found you. When you think of your wife, not only are you excited about your future, but you have no intentions on ever returning to the women from your past.

What you've just done for yourself and for your lady is you've upgraded the relationship, and that is a sure sign of growth. First you started out as friends, then dating, then a couple, then engaged, and then marriage. The relationship is constantly growing, reaching new heights and the sky is the limit. If you're starting to get bored, all that means is you're not actively working towards continually upgrading the relationship. There is so much you can do to add value to your marriage like have children, adopt children, exercise, travel the world, start a new business, just to name a few.

That's the beauty of a marriage, you get to upgrade different facets of your life with someone who actually signed up for it. Together you will figure out how to keep a roof over your head, clothes on your back, food on your table and romance in the bedroom. It will give you peace of mind having this security in your relationship which will allow you to be a better man, a better husband, a better father and a better leader. Lacking discipline when it comes to relationships is something that holds many men back from being successful in life. So much time, energy, effort and money is wasted trying to conquer *women*, that he never masters the art of being *with a* woman.

Women of substance don't look to marry just anything, they have standards, and after building yourself up to be a quality man of substance you're going to be more than ready to meet her standards. There's no need to feel pressured into getting married, I'm simply sharing the value that comes with it. Marriage isn't for everybody, marriage is only for the ready. If you're going to make a life-long commitment, build yourself up first so that you'll have the knowledge, the skills and the tools you need to maintain it. Happy wife, happy life!

Introduce Her To Your Family & Friends

I love spending time with my family because it's a great opportunity to just relax and be myself. This time together is sacred, and not everyone is welcome to join the circle. I value their opinions, I respect their homes and their privacy, and the feelings are mutual. When the holidays come around, and it's time to reunite, everyone brings their significant other and their kids, and if they're single they bring themselves. If a woman was invited to a family function, that meant she was somebody important, and she knows it.

I had a frriend back in college (Lane) who was dating a woman who had a young child, she modeled as a hobby and I believe she was a student as well. I didn't have to meet her to know that she wasn't the one, I simply deduced based on the information he had given me. I was going to school in Texas so when the holidays came around, I would go back home to New York, but would inquire as to what his plans were. He would go on to tell me about all the delicious food his family was planning on making and the relatives he would connect with, but made no mention of his lady. This was no surprise to me because I already knew that she wasn't someone he was taking seriously for a multitude of reasons.

I would soon meet her and sure enough she was a beauty on the outside, but I didn't see the value on the inside. It was now clearer to me *why* he kept her around his circle, but didn't invite her in it. She was good enough for him to invite to bed, but not good enough to invite back home. Months and years had passed and the holidays came back around, and I would ask him *again* what are your plans. And he would say the same thing about visiting family, a smorgasbord of food, and the whole nine, but no invite for the lady.

We would talk; laugh and joke, and then we somehow started talking about his mom and then his girlfriend. So I asked him, "Have you ever introduced her to your mom" and he replied "Hell no!" I was 22 at the time so forgive me, but we both laughed hysterically because we knew what that meant for *her*. To be in a relationship with someone for 2+ years, and have not met the most important people in a man's life (particularly his mother/sister), that says a lot about the relationship. Obviously, that also said a lot about Lane.

He was wasting this poor woman's time, and leading her to believe that she was someone of significance knowing full well that she wasn't. Poor girl, I'm sure she wanted to feel significant, she wanted to meet his family, but simply didn't know how to require it. 8 years later, neither one of them are together and have pursued new people. Hopefully she learned a valuable lesson about the value of her time. Lane got the best of her, but at the same time, he showed the worst of him and that's nothing to be proud of.

There's no value in stringing women along and wasting their time because your time is being wasted too. Not only are you blocking her from meeting someone that values her, but you are also blocking yourself from meeting someone that *you* value. On the one hand, she's foolish for falling into the trap, but on the other hand, you're at fault for setting it. Women look to men for leadership, and that's nothing you should look to take advantage of. This could be your daughter, your sister, or your mother who's being led astray by someone else.

When it comes to dating and relationships, you have to think long-term. Right from the moment you meet her you should give her a thorough evaluation. Ask yourself some questions like: Could I wake up to her every morning for the rest of my life? Would I want to introduce her to my mother? Is this someone I would want to have children with? Keep these questions in the back of your mind as we lead up to them in a moment.

Before you get anywhere with a woman, you've got to check her out and see what she's about. Is she confident, does she have high-esteem, is she ambitious, is she courageous, is she educated, is she goal and career oriented? The standards and requirements for dating differ from person to person, but you should look for the things you like up-front. This will help you determine whether or not you should move forward. If she passed the test, then it's time to get started with the pursuit.

Walk up to her and introduce yourself, and get a feel of her energy. Did she receive you well, is she open to conversation, does she seem genuinely interested, is she reluctant to give information? Hopefully you were able to walk out of there with her contact information and can get to know her a little better. Remember, this is your life we're talking about, your legacy, and you're doing your due diligence to find a suitable partner. Hopefully this partner is going to be introduced not only to your family, but also to the world.

Too often do we skip over the process called "Getting To Know Each Other" which results in getting yourselves emotionally involved prematurely. Instead, take your time, do it right so that won't have any future regrets. If you're investing your time in it, and you are devoted to it, you should be proud to announce it from the mountaintops. If you feel the need to hide it or you are ashamed of it, perhaps you shouldn't be involved in it. Sure, it's easy to connect with someone when it's convenient, but at what cost?

I grew up with 5 brothers and 1 sister, and many male cousins, and even as a child I knew that when a man brings a woman home, she's *significant*. It would bring shame to my mom if my brothers brought home random women to our family gatherings. "What kind of men did I raise" would be the thoughts crossing her mind. For me, bringing a woman home was a proud moment; it was a sign that I was committed and trying out this whole relationship thing. The first time I brought a woman home to my mom, I was a freshman in college.

I was 18 years old and this was my first *real* relationship. We were both student athletes, but she was a senior, had a great job, her own car, but more importantly she was into me. I thought I was the MAN! Here I am, the new kid on the block and I managed to snatch up a senior in college who was quite in demand herself. I snatched her up quick and by the summer, I introduced her to my mother.

At that age, I didn't know what I was doing as it pertains to relationships; I just got out of an 18 year relationship with my parents. The point is I wanted to show my girlfriend at the time how I felt about her. I felt she was important enough to meet the people who were important to me. My mother liked her, but then again my mother likes everybody. My brothers liked her and she was liked at our school too.

Were we going to get married and live happily ever after? Probably not, I was too uncertain about my own future at that age, let alone a future with a woman. I was simply putting into practice the treatment I felt the woman in my life deserved. She also introduced me to her family, and I felt it was an appropriate gesture. My family is an important staple in my life, so when the right women comes along and proves herself worthy, it only makes sense for them to meet.

Your lady wants to meet that best friend you can't stop talking about, or joking with over the phone. She wants to meet your child that you can't stop bragging about. She wants to be invited over for Thanksgiving and Christmas dinner with the family and treated like she's a part of the family. She wants to be able to interact and communicate with your family members without you being around. She wants to feel as though you are planning to make her an official part of your family.

Your time is the most valuable thing you have in this world, but know that your time is limited. Not only is your time limited on this earth, but a woman will only give you so much of her time before she realizes you are wasting it. She wants to feel as if she is a part of something special, and that will require you to show her more than just you. She wants to be included in things that are near and dear to your heart. And more importantly, she wants to be given a title.

Marriage Is A Full-Time Job

Anytime I talk to a client about marriage, I like to equate the union to a business. Marriage is a full-time job and requires a lot of work, which is why I admire those who have taken this step and are still together. It's a new stage of life that requires a lot of change, and quite frankly can be scary for someone who's been single for their entire life. Not only do you have to try and figure out what *you're* going through emotionally, but now you have to consider someone *else's* feelings too… FOREVER! If you're considering getting married, know that the idea is for it to last a lifetime.

My mother was married to my father before I even came out of the womb; he passed away when I was only one year old, but by the time I was old enough to identify people by their names (it seemed), she was married again. Mostly all of my aunts and uncles were married, and I got a pretty good grasp of what it meant to be married growing up. I looked at it as a *bond* between two people that could only be separated by the two people who formed it. They would keep to themselves and only share information that they agreed was *for* the public.

It's a challenging lifestyle change as it demands a great deal of your time, energy and focus, but it has its benefits. That's why I say marriage isn't for everybody; marriage is only for the *ready*. When I think of marriage, I look at it as an upgrade to every relationship you've experienced in your past. The difference is, this is the one relationship that you don't quit on or walk away from when times get rough. This is the relationship that you roll up your sleeves and repair the damage that's been done, and you do it *together*.

In my line of work, I meet countless people who are in marriages and are trying to get out for various reasons. Often times, the reasons are small, but at the same time are huge. I once spoke with a woman who was married to a man in the military; she was young and had a child by him. She explained to me that he was a great guy, he did everything for her and the baby, and the problem was that she simply wasn't attracted to him. Her reason for marrying him was to benefit from his benefits. On the one hand, he's overseas protecting our country and looking forward to coming back to the U.S. to embrace his wife and family. On the other hand, she's back at home and miserable because she didn't plan on living out the marriage she entered into.

Countless divorces take place for similar reasons and will continue to rise if you go into it not planning to do the work to make it last. Yes, it's a sacrifice of your time, resources, body and soul, but that's what marriage is all about. Your willingness to be selfless for the benefit of your wife is what will make her love you til death. Once you start loving, you can't stop, otherwise you'll cause conflict in areas where they should be resolutions. The same time, energy, and effort you put into your job in order to stay relevant is equivalent to how you should approach your marriage.

If you show up late to work or don't show up at all, the boss will for sure call you into the office to discuss this change in behavior. Your value to the company depends on your ability to produce at the company. If you stop producing at the company, then before long they will no longer require your services. Being in a marriage is no different; your value in the marriage depends on your ability to produce in the marriage. If you stop producing in the marriage, before long she will no longer require your services.

It sounds a little harsh, but it's true. We only have one life to live and no one wants to spend a lifetime with someone who isn't willing to put in the work to make him or her happy. Just imagine that your favorite thing about your wife is for her to cook, and she stops cooking for months on end… You'll be miserable and looking for a way to get out of it. The marriage is only fun if both parties are doing what they are supposed to be doing to make it work. This is why getting to know each other is so important because you get to see where one another's strengths and weaknesses lie.

You don't want to wait until you're married to get to know your wife. She should already be a wife before you meet her and *that* needs to be the reason you fall in love with her. If she wasn't wife material when you met her, she certainly won't miraculously change into a wife after you marry her. When you take the time to get to know her, she'll express her morals and values, and from there you can do the same. You then can decide whether or not this is someone you would like to build with based on her values.

Your values combined have to be strong enough for the two of you to hold onto and use as a standard for your growth and prosperity. If a woman doesn't have a strong value system, chances are you won't truly value *her*. What that does to the marriage is it causes you to view her as unworthy, which will impact your desire to perform as a suitable husband. In the event that you settle on a woman with poor values, you must take responsibility for making that choice. You're the leader, and should take pride in having the knowledge and wisdom to make good choices for yourself and for those who depend on you.

When you're single, there isn't much pressure because there's no one particular woman who is depending on you. In a marriage, your wife is depending on you and you are depending on her. She expects you to protect her against any force or enemy at all cost. She expects you to provide for her, be her source of entertainment, and her shoulder to cry on. If nobody else is there for her, it should be *you*; this is what you signed up for and this is what you are expected to do.

Get excited about your marriage; having someone there for you through thick and thin is a wonderful thing. Part of the reason why many relationships are broken and are breaking is because there's no sense of loyalty. Since there's no legally binding contract keeping them together, they simply walk away when times get rough. Being able to see the same face each and everyday when you're up and when you're down is a blessing that many people *wish* they had. It's something that a lot of us men secretly aspire to have, but most are simply not ready for.

There are a lot of men who have been blessed with the gift of marriage, but unfortunately don't treat it as if it's a gift. They take it for granted because they feel as though the woman they married isn't going anywhere. In fact, *these* types of brothers still haven't come to understand the true value of marriage; they simply got married for *her*. For him, nothing has changed, same friends, same heart, same mind, and the same ways. He appreciates the convenience of a marriage, but doesn't value the sanctity of the marriage.

His attitude towards his marriage is what will cause it to fall apart. If a marriage isn't built on love, it will eventually crumble. Have you ever gone to the customer service area of a store only to find a representative who has absolutely no desire to serve the customers? I have, and the first thing that comes to mind is, "If you don't like to serve customers, why apply for and accept a customer service position?". The answer is quite simple, they didn't apply to and accept the job to better the company, they applied and accepted the job to better themselves. Meanwhile they are hurting the company because repeat business depends heavily on the customer service provided by the company.

The same applies to a marriage, no one is forcing you to get into it, but if you make that choice, put in the work. The success of the marriage depends on you and your partner's diligence and it simply cannot thrive without it. You should want to be your wife's everything so that she won't have to depend on another man for anything. When your wife is in need, she should turn to you, and you should be there to deliver. Morning, noon, or night you should be readily available and accessible to her.

Be proud of your title as a husband because not a lot of men have it, in fact not a lot of men deserve it, and that's what makes you unique. You are one of the many who was brave enough to commit to a life-long journey with someone and that is a great honor. In order for you to continue to be held to these high regards, you must stand by your wife, be loyal and faithful. You must remember your vows and stay committed to them and you embark on this new territory. Marriage isn't for everybody but it will be for you if you are strong enough to fight until the end of time to keep it alive.

Many great things will come from your hard work and dedication as a husband. You'll have the opportunity to spend countless birthdays and holidays with your beloved wife, bear children and raise them together. You'll be able to take pride in presenting your lady to the world as your wife. You'll be a beam of hope and light to the many who aspire to take on the challenge of marriage. Best of all you will be able to give and receive all benefits of staying on the job with the woman you love.

If You Love Her, Put A Ring On It

Life is all about building relationships and leaving behind legacies, so lets talk about yours for a moment. After you leave this earth, you want people to remember your spirit, and the way you do that is through your legacy. Some men do this through their career, some through family, while others do neither. The last thing you want to do is live your life and have nothing to show for it. No, you want to have assets to leave your children, memories for your family, and a legacy for the world.

For the average guy, one of our main priorities in life is to get closer to a woman. We go to school so that we can get a better education, leading to a better job and hopefully more money. That money can afford us a nice place to live, nice cars, clothes and buying power. We hope that these things will attract more women no matter how shallow it may seem. And this brings about the problem; our desire to attract *women* instead of *a* woman.

As we grow older and begin to mature, we then realize that there isn't much value in having multiple women. As sure as you are able to access these multiple women, your time, energy, and effort is divided among them. You started out strong; you were educated, career oriented, independent, and ready to pursue a woman. Once you found a woman, she wasn't enough for you because you wanted to have it all. It's not that she wasn't a great woman; the fact is that you weren't ready to receive her.

Now, I totally understand your fascination with women, they are truly amazing. They listen to your problems and help you find solutions, they're resourceful, and know how to make a man feel good (if you know what I mean). Sounds like a keeper to me; get it? Keep her! Sometimes though when you meet an amazing woman, you might be at a point in *your* life when you're not so amazing.

Believe me, we've all been there and that drives women crazy! It boggles their minds how they could offer you the world and you still won't offer them a ring. Or better yet, you offer them rings of rubber, but never a ring of promise. It affects their self-esteem and ruins their confidence because they're giving you their best, and you're not reciprocating. That's not fair to them, and you know it.

You have to keep your partner motivated. Your relationship is no different from the principles found at a job. You wouldn't want to stay in the mail room for 2, 5 and 10 years knowing that you are smart, capable and deserving of a higher position. It's insulting to be kept on the ground level when you've done so much to add value to the company. Before long you'll be forced to quit because it's no longer worth it to stay.

That's exactly how women feel when they don't get the ring. Women aren't dating for their health, they want to build a future with someone and be exclusive. They'll do anything for you just as they would from the mailroom at a company, just so long as you give them a promotion. That promotion from the mailroom is the equivalent to a girlfriend status. She's not the CEO or the wife, but she's working her way up.

Keep your woman motivated by showing her that you want her to have a stake in your life. Otherwise, your company will soon be filing for bankruptcy. It doesn't take a bunch of women to take care of your heart's desires. In fact, if you need more than one woman, that insists you haven't found the right "one". You haven't found the right one because you're not focused. Either that or you're simply not mature enough to be loyal.

There comes a time in every man's life where he's going to have to show and prove that he is able to commit to *someone*. Relationships aren't for everybody; relationships are only for the *ready*! Perhaps you've met an amazing woman who compliments you and you're working towards something now. This is great if you're serious about building with her. Don't waste a woman's time if you have no intentions of building a future with her.

One of the things that many women fear is missing the opportunity to bear children (also known as the biological clock). As they begin to reach a certain age, life and relationships becomes more serious for them, and they don't want to waste valuable time dating aimlessly. For men, we are fortunate to have more time than women to have children and as many as we want. All we have to do is seek out younger and more fertile women. Nonetheless, we should be considerate of these concerns if we are investing time in a woman.

From one man to another, we know from day one if we're going to marry a woman. Sometimes, it's simply her curvaceous body that attracted us, or her money, or her resources. There's not a chance in hell that she's going to be your wife and you know it. Yet and still, you do things like date, sleep together, and introduce her to family, etc as if she's somebody significant. In her mind, she thinks she's going places, but in your mind, you know the only place you want to take her is to bed.

Now, I understand, a man has needs, but taking advantage of a woman by playing with her emotions isn't a *need*. This is you being selfish and going after what you want. What you *need* is exactly the woman you have, you simply don't appreciate her. You don't appreciate her because of the man you currently are; you aren't acting with integrity, you're acting selfishly. You've got your cake and you're eating it too.

Have we forgotten the story about the mailroom worker already? It's only a matter of time before she puts in her two-week notice. She'd be a fool to stay with you and allow herself to be used with nothing to show for it. She wants a promotion; a title, a commitment, a ring! She wants you to show signs that you value and appreciate her and that you want her around.

The first year was the icebreaker; you're just getting to know one another and are a little nervous about introducing her to your family, ok fine. The second year, she's starting to feel left out and is wondering where she stands with you. The third year it's insulting to her character and she's beginning to lose her respect for you as a man because you don't truly acknowledge her as your woman. Sure, you call her all types of pet names, you spend more time with her than any other woman, and people suspect that you're at least sleeping together, but *you* haven't shown any signs of commitment.

It's like playing on the Varsity basketball at the college level and being "red shirted". Red shirted? That's an entire year of your life that you could've invested someplace else, and instead you're on the sidelines pretending to be happy that your teammates have established a commitment. If you see value in her, put her in the game and keep her off the sidelines and off the bench. Let the world know that this is the woman you want to spend the rest of your life with.

Your lady is in your life because you are significant to her; she's open to giving you her all, but first she wants you to show her that you *want* her all. She will know that you have interest in what she has to offer based on your proposal. Your actions speak louder than words; when you present a ring, you're making a promise. When you withhold the ring, you are showing that you don't feel she's worth the promise. Take the relationship to the next level by putting a proposal on the table. If you love her, put a ring on her.

Marriage Is An Upgrade

When I was a kid growing up, I recall spending a lot of time with my family. On special occasions such as holidays, birthdays, etc. we would all gather at a selected family member's house and celebrate. Typically, it would be The Bostock's/Smith's which consisted of myself, my siblings, my mom and my step-dad, the Wallace's, the Stewart's, and the Cornish's. What I grew up seeing in each family was a husband, wife and kids; no one family was perfect, but they were all stronger when they stuck together. Seeing such family values displayed at such a young age gave us something to model after as adults.

I always thought to myself that I would want to have the same amount of kids my parents had (5 or 6). Now that I've had my first child, I simply want to have as many as I could afford. Lol It was fun growing up with 5 brothers and 1 sister; I don't know how my parents managed to give us everything that we wanted and needed, but they did it and I couldn't be more proud of them. There was a time or two when my mom and step-dad separated, but when they got back together, my mother was literally glowing. She would cook more, sing more and smile more and I knew my step-dad had a lot to do with it.

I'm quite sure that if there were no value in the marriage, my step-dad would've never come back. I mean we weren't the best step-kids in the world, but we certainly weren't the worst, and we loved having him around. My step-dad was without a doubt a "yes man", and in many ways that worked in his favor. The saying goes "Happy Wife, Happy life!". My mom would make a special request, (one of many) and he would figure out a way to get it done. They were perfect for each other I suppose, my step-dad needed something to do, and my mom needed someone to do it.

In a marriage, there are certain requirements that need to be met in order for it to work. Of course there are certain gender roles that should be taken into consideration, but outside of that, each individual may have their own personal preferences. For example, as a man, you may feel it's a deal breaker if a woman doesn't know how to cook. For a woman, it may be a deal breaker if you don't know how to fix things. Figuring out what that *thing* is for your wife and mastering it will not only add value to the marriage, but it will also add peace to the marriage.

Typically speaking, it's women who look forward to the wedding, but men certainly appreciate the value in a marriage. Most men are simply too afraid to risk their name and reputation on such high stakes. They feel as if they're going to lose something from making a life-long commitment. The great thing about marriage is, you're not giving up your independence, but rather gaining interdependence. It's the beginning of a new period in your life, and the end of and old one.

People ask me all the time "Cheyenne, you seem to have the principles of relationships all figured out, why aren't you married?" The answer is simple and I'm sure many of you can relate. Marriage isn't for everybody; marriage is only for the *ready*. The next time someone asks you, "Why aren't you married?", reply simply by saying, "I'm not married because I'm single! I can only claim one relationship status at a time.". Marriage is forever, so the preparation for the marriage is equally as important as the actual marriage.

When I think of marriage, the words that come to mind are "protect, provide and serve". In order to handle this job, you will need to be strong enough spiritually, physically and emotionally to protect your family. These are things that you can accomplish while you are single and working on building yourself up as a man. A woman will feel secure in knowing that your strength goes beyond the physical and into the spiritual. Being in good physical health gives her confidence of knowing you will be around to also protect your family physically. Your portrayal of humility and servitude shows your ability to be an effective leader.

Marriage is an investment, not only of your money, but also of your time, energy and resources. It's a man's role to provide for his family; you won't need money to get the girl, but you *will* need money to keep her. There's the cost of food to consider, shelter, clothing, health and dental insurance, life insurance as well as many other unforeseen expenses. Now, don't be afraid, taking care of others is a part of life; you're a man, you are built for this. If you've never experienced taking care of others and providing for others, start practicing.

The key to a successful marriage is taking steps to plan and prepare for longevity. Instead of looking at all of the expenses that are associated with marriage as a liability, start looking at them as assets. When you wake up in the morning and see your beautiful wife and kids, you'll go that much harder at work because you know that the funds are going to a great cause. Now that you have a wife and family, you're more health conscious because you want to be there for them. Providing for others has helped you become more financially responsible, and better at budgeting money. Your time is spent more wisely now because the people you love are waiting for you to share it.

It's so easy to be selfish when you're not obligated to share your time, energy, money and resources with anyone. In a marriage, you're expected to be selfless and do the exact opposite. Not everyone is able to do make this sacrifice, and for many it will take some time, but before long, settling down will eventually come to pass. The random sex partners, late night parties and binge drinking gets old and so will you. In fact, those things never brought a man happiness to begin with; they are simply ways to forget about the areas we are lacking.

Once you reach a certain level of maturity, you will begin to not only see more value in women, but you'll also see more value in yourself. You will take greater pride in getting to know a woman because *now*, you are dating with a different purpose in mind. You've already experienced one nightstands, friends with benefits, and relationships that were convenient but weren't a priority. The one thing that they all had in common was they lacked substance. You knew deep in your heart when you first met them that they would never meet your mother, have your child or bear your last name, you were simply biding time until you got your life together.

Every man wants the benefits of a marriage, (i.e. Food, Sex And Peace Of Mind), but most aren't willing to invest or can't afford what it costs to have a wife and a family. There's a reason why you are attracted to women whom you feel aren't worthy, and it's because you yourself aren't yet worthy. You haven't built yourself up enough to be a qualified candidate for marriage, and you know it, so you settle for women who aren't worthy as well. You'll be the perfect match for her for as long as you choose to remain on that level. The moment you decide to upgrade yourself and improve yourself, you'll start to attract more quality women of substance.

Of course you don't want to marry her, she's just as broke as you are. Of course you won't introduce her to your mother, you met her at a bar and slept with her on the 1st night; not only does it speak to *her* character, but it also speaks to yours. Indeed you're ashamed to introduce her to your friends because she's ridiculously out of shape, but the *real* reason you settled for her is because *you* too are out of shape and can't complain. It's no wonder you've been living with her for years, even had a child together and still haven't asked for her hand in marriage, you have no plans for your own future, let alone a future with *her*.

It's time to take control of your life and start taking steps towards self-improvement. Marriage is without a doubt a blessing, but can be a curse if you are not prepared for what comes with it. My grandfather

Francis H. Bostock Sr met my grandmother Ethel Novella Epps in the spring of 1942, and they got married the following summer. They lived happily together in Brooklyn, NY and were married for almost fifty-two years. My grandparents are long gone, but it's something that I'm still proud of today. I'm sure they've had marriage and money problems just like any other, but they loved each other enough to face them together.

In today's times, people are getting divorced just a couple of years, months, and even weeks after the marriage. Before getting into a marriage, come up with a way to define it. To me, marriage means "coming together, fighting together and staying together." Growing up, I've had quite a few friends, but not all of them would help fight my battles, and not all of them are still around today. On the day I get married, I foresee looking into the eyes of a woman who is like no other woman from my past, but the woman I need in my future. She will be someone I want to be with, fight for, and stay with until death.

After a certain age, you no longer want to be known as "The Bachelor", you want to be known as "The Husband", "The Father", or "The Family Man". That makes sense because that's what maturity is all about; most men simply haven't reached that point in their lives yet. Being a husband will bring out the best in you if you are willing to let go of the worst of you. Take pride in honoring a woman through marriage, building a legacy and raising a family by God's standards. If you show a woman that are you are capable of leading, providing, protecting and serving, she will do everything in her power to support you. Let her upgrade you!

Til Death Do You Part

Every time I go to a wedding I find myself chuckling on the inside when the priest gets to the "Til death do you part" part of the sermon. It's one of those "Are you SURE you want to do this?" moments. Lol I imagine that particular moment to be a nervous one because once you say, "I do", you're declaring before God and witnesses that you are in it for the long haul. This is a moment that is literally going to change your life forever!

I suppose that's what makes it so scary for so many people; it's not the word *marriage* that scares them, it's the word *change*. Everything that you're used to has to change for the sake of your marriage, and sometimes that can be a good thing. Sometimes we do things wrong our entire lives, and because we've been doing it wrong for so long, we are convinced that it's right. Sometimes change is exactly the thing we need in order to finally get it right. At times our pride won't allow us to admit that our way isn't working, isn't fruitful or isn't productive.

What a marriage offers is another perspective from someone who genuinely cares. I don't know about you, but the person I spend the rest of my life with has to genuinely care about my thoughts, feelings, passion and my pain. I couldn't imagine sharing a life with someone who takes no interest in the things that interest me. I've committed to many things in my life and what mattered the most was the end results. If I'm working hard on a basketball team, I want to win a championship. If I'm putting forth my time, energy, effort and money into college, I want to earn a degree.

The same applies to my marriage, if I'm committed to a woman for a lifetime I want her knowledge, resources, love and support forever and ever. This is why it's extremely important to know who you are, and know who you're dealing with. If you choose wrong, you could end up miserable forever and ever. You want to be in a union with someone that you value and who also values you, so be sure to take your time before making this crucial life changing decision.

My grandparents on my father's side were married for 50+ years until my grandmother passed away in 1995. My grandfather passed away in 2004 and at that age, I was too young to even think about marriage, let alone the value of it. If he were alive to day I would ask him questions about his values, what made him fall in love with my grandmother, and what kept them together for so long. If I had to guess, I would say that it was pure unfiltered love. They loved each other enough to stay together, value each other, and set an example for generations to come.

They were always pleasant around one another, it was as if they knew exactly what the other wanted out of life, and allowed each other to enjoy it. My grandmother was a smoker, and she eventually died of cancer at an old age. My grandfather never belittled my grandmother or bashed her for habit of smoking (not in front of us anyway). I would imagine that he came to terms with this was a habit she was unwilling to give up, and that he would have to live with. That's a beautiful thing when two people are able to accept each other with their flaws and all and still love them to death.

Like most men, my grandfather didn't do too much talking, but he did a lot of doing. He was consistent with his behavior when we came around. He would ask us questions about school, set a bowl of candy out for us, prepare dinner before we arrived and then took us to the park where he would take candid photos of us. Everyone needs an escape from home from time to time and for an old man, this was the perfect opportunity. My grandfather was really calm, cool and *sometimes* a little grouchy, and perhaps the grouchy part was something that my grandmother had to get over.

There building had a wonderful view of the Williamsburg bridge in Brooklyn, and we loved to look at the night's skyline as kids. I would imagine that that was something my grandparents enjoyed doing as well. They had 3 sons and a host of grandchildren and great grandchildren that they could be proud of. They had done something with their lives that would never be forgotten. They built a relationship with one another and left behind a legacy in this world, and they did it all *together*.

If there's nothing else I admired about my grandparents, it's definitely their values for marriage. We all will face the day when we are no longer able to write a book, give a speech, or pass down a tradition with our words. Our actions throughout the courses of our lives in many cases will be all the lessons that future generations will need to learn and grow. I can't sit here and say that my grandfather never taught me anything about marriage simply because he never spoke of it. He taught me the value of marriage by standing by his wife until she took her last breath.

That's not something you see everyday, especially in this day in age where people are walking in and out of marriages like a revolving door. I would like to think of marriage as a final destination; you've stopped everywhere else and now it's time to settle down. I would imagine that people such as my grandparents who have been married for so long had to make a few stops before hand. There's nothing wrong with exploring the world, traveling, meeting new people and enjoying the single life first. In fact, it's highly recommended; doing so will allow you to see the value in the trade-off from single to married life.

Look forward to building your first home, and one day sharing it with someone special. Look forward to traveling the world, trying new things and meeting new people, and plan to one day do these things with your wife and family. Look forward to partnering in business with your wife and making future investments together. Look forward to sharing your time, resources, love and money with your wife. View marriage as a life-long investment and plan to be married until death.

Throughout the course of your life, you will meet many people who will come and go. Some will leave because they didn't belong there in the first place, some will leave because they've found someone more worthy of their time, and some will feel they have no further use for you. Life is about building relationships and leaving behind legacies; the more valuable you are to a person, the more they will want you around. When you focus your energy in one area at a time, you can yield the greatest results. By choosing someone that you promise to spend the rest of your life with, you are able the channel everything in your power towards their happiness, and that's the best way to keep a wife. Happy wife, happy life!

Of my two best friends, one of them is married, has two daughters and appears to be very happy. They've been together for over 5 years and I'm happy to see that they're progressing. I'm extremely proud because I know where he used to be in life, and now I see a better man than he ever was. Like any other marriage, they have ups and downs, but they are going through the motions *together*. When I see him post pictures and messages about his family on Facebook it makes me proud to see that he's being the quality man of substance that his wife and family deserves.

Anytime a married client comes to me for advice, I don't offer them a way out; I offer them a way right back in. The only way to work it out is to simply work it out. That's what being loyal to a marriage is all about, finding the inner strength, the desire and the self-discipline to sustain the union until death. If you walk away from everything in your life that falls apart or isn't working, you'll never acquire the knowledge of how to fix things. Loyalty may be a small word but it's a BIG thing.

It's easy to just walk away, and if you're looking for something that is easy, marriage isn't it. Ask anyone who's been married or is married and they will tell you that it's hard work. In fact, this may be one of the hardest things you'll ever have to do in life, but the best part is you won't have to do it alone. You'll have a partner who will be there when you laugh, when you cry, when you're up and when you're down. You'll have someone to create new memories with and to cherish the old ones.

Being loyal to your marriage will build character not only in you but also in everyone around you. Your friends will look at you as a beam of hope and will aspire to one day have a partner for life. Your children will respect you for getting it right, showing discipline and being an active part of the family as a whole. Your family and your community will commend you on your diligence and celebrate with you every year and you'll honor your anniversary. When you are gone, the people who remember you will speak about the things you valued in life and your marriage will be right at the top of that list.

Chapter 6:

Fatherhood

Get Ready To Be A Father

When I was growing up, I've always had a love for babies, especially the ones with big, fat, chubby cheeks. They were so full of love, joy and happiness and it seemed like nothing could take that away from them. I enjoyed taking the time to understand certain behavior patterns. For example when they needed a change, when they were hungry, or simply when they wanted to play. They were harmless and wanted nothing more than to be loved, kind of like me. At the time, I knew that I loved sharing moments with the adorable babies in my family, but I by no means was ready to be a father.

When I was 12, my niece Atiyana was born and I enjoyed watching her grow. Six years later my nephew Milton Jr. was born and he looked a bit like me. I was 17 and had just moved in with my eldest brother Milton Sr. and his family, so I got to spend a lot of time with my baby nephew. I would dress him up, take him places and tell people that he was my son. When I would leave the house to go to school, "Little Milton" would cry his eyes out and then go to the window so that I could see and hear him crying from outside.

I knew that one day I would make a good dad, but I by no means was ready to take that step. I was young, still wet behind the ears and quite frankly was a baby myself. And besides, my focus was on basketball. Ok let's be honest, my focus was also on women too, but basketball was my main focus. I had to stay focused on my goals because I wanted to play college basketball and I didn't want to pay for it.

After winning the state championship two years in a row (2001-2002) at Saint Anthony high school, I graduated and moved back to Texas to be amongst my immediate family members and friends. I attended Texas Wesleyan University, continued to play basketball and met lots of wonderful new people. I was the new kid from New York on campus and I loved the attention. I also met two of my best friends while at college and they were just as popular. We partied, drank, fraternized and needless to say, I was by no means ready to be a father.

For the first time in my life, I was away from my parents, away from my siblings and away from anyone who was emotionally connected to me. I felt so FREE and I didn't want to give up that freedom anytime soon. No curfew, no limits, no rules! I had my little dorm room, my unlimited meal bucks, and was surrounded by women who were also on a "freedom high" and wanted to enjoy it just like me. The on campus college life was like heaven!

During the holidays, I would go back to New York to visit family and friends, and one year my cousin hosted a Christmas party and invited his friends to join. I arrived, single and ready to mingle, rang the doorbell and when the door opened, there she stood. All I could hear in my head was Biggie Smalls saying "I see some ladies tonight who should be havin' my baby... Baby!". I was 21, and she was 26, and I've always been into older women because they seemed to be more mature and more established than the women my age. Furthermore, a more seasoned woman would have higher expectations of me and that gave me more motivation to work harder to maintain the relationship with them. Even with that said, and at age 21, I was by no means ready to be in a relationship, let alone a father.

Finally, I was old enough to drink "responsibly" or at least legally, I could get into clubs without a fake I.D. and older women would respect me as an and official adult (so I thought). I felt like I had finally become a man and would enjoy it for a little bit. I was in a relationship during the latter part of my freshmen year of college, but *this* would be my longest relationship ever. We did the long distance thing, she would come visit me in Texas and I would come visit her in NJ. The distance, plus the time we spent apart made the relationship that much more intriguing.

One day as I'm hanging out with my two best friends, I get a yahoo instant message asking me to accept a file. It was a picture from my *then* girlfriend showing me a positive pregnancy test. I didn't know how to feel or how to react at that moment; I was a junior in college, never married, no kids, no felonies, and making a name for myself with my photography business. I responded cheerfully to let her know that I was happy about the results, but on the inside I was nervous about the results. One moment, I thought to myself, "Alright!!! I'm about to be a father" then the next I thought "WOAH!!! I'm about to be a father?"

My whole life up until now was all about me, Me, ME! Maybe this was exactly what I needed to get me out of selfish mode and start living for a greater purpose. I didn't have a house, a car, or steady cash flow to raise this child with, but what I came to realize was, being a father isn't about "presents" it's about presence. No matter how much you shower your child with money and gifts, what your child will value the most is that you're *there*. Your child wants you to be there when you're rich, when you're poor, when you're up and when you're down. They only care about the opportunity to have a relationship with you.

A positive, long-lasting relationship with anyone will require some discomfort, it will require an investment and it will require great sacrifice. I was in my final year at Texas Wesleyan University and I had just gotten back from summer vacation with my *then* pregnant girlfriend. I had registered for all of my classes, gotten comfortable in my apartment and then I get "the call". It was 10 o'clock at night, I had just gotten in from an event and she said, "I can't wait any longer, this baby is coming. You have to come back now!".

At that moment, I thought I was going to become another statistic, another black college dropout making babies. I refused to accept that and told her "I'm on the next flight back home". I had to withdraw from school, and enroll in a local NJ college for a semester, but it was all worth it because I got to spend the first 5 months of my son's life with him instead of away from him. The next semester I transferred back to Texas Wesleyan University where I graduated along side of my two best friends and my son and his mother were both there to witness it.

There's already enough pressure being young, black and finishing college, and one of my fears was letting everyone down. When I graduated high school, I had to accept the fact that I had to move on and do something different. I may not have had all of the necessary funds, knowledge or skills to make it through college, but I managed to acquire these things as I went along. I looked at fatherhood the same way; I could learn how to excel at my new life simply by taking one step at a time and progressing. Failure simply means that you've given up on succeeding, so the only way to not be a good father is if you stop trying.

In life, not everything will go according to planned; sometimes you have to make adjustments based on your circumstances. We are made for this, built to rise to any occasion and not simply survive in it, but also overcome it. When that baby comes, you will be a father whether you accept that title or not, and your child well forever look to you to be their dad. Having a child just might be the push you need to be responsible, to work harder, to love more and care about others. Instead of shying away from this great responsibility, embrace it and watch how much value it adds to your life.

It will give you a greater sense of purpose knowing that you're not stretching your mind trying to think of your next big idea simply for your own benefit, you're doing it to create a better life for your family. You'll take pride in eating healthier and taking better care of your body *now* because you want to live long enough to watch your child grow up and have kids of their own. Your maturity level will shine through when you'd much rather have movie night at home with the family on Saturday then party at the club until Sunday with your boys. And wait until your child learns to walk, talk and further express their feelings, you'll be just as in love with them as they are with you. Caring for others and being responsible builds character and will do wonders for your life as a man.

Preparing for fatherhood is about being emotionally available enough to give love and receive it. No child asks to be born into this world, they were all brought here, and it's your responsibility to raise the children you make. Children need emotional support as well as financial support so be prepared emotionally and financially to provide. Furthermore, your duties as a parent don't discontinue after a break-up; your duties as a father carry on for life. Even if you and the child's mother aren't together anymore, you should always be together in spirit for the sake of the child.

Your health is important and will have a huge impact on the level by which you are able to interact with your child. Your child will be young and full of life and will want you to engage and interact with them physically and emotionally. They will want to ride on your shoulders, have you spin them around, race them for miles, and the play fighting never gets old. Being in great physical shape will not only do wonders for your life, but it will also add tremendous value to the lives of your children.

Use discernment when choosing someone to have a child with because having a child is a life-long commitment. Make your best effort to have children with someone you love and can tolerate. The happier you are about your choice, the better you will treat yourself, the mother and the child. Peace of mind is the most important thing to have, especially in the home; it sets the tone by which you interact with others outside of the home. Be the best man you can be and you'll attract the best woman, have the best relationship, and raise the best child. Be prepared!

Plan To Be A Better Father

For years a man can live his life irresponsibly, and for a while, it's exciting and feels worthwhile to live life without a worry or a care. But there comes a time in every man's life where he decides he wants *more* for his life and his legacy, he wants to contribute to society and add value to the lives of others. These epiphanies normally come when he's experienced some sort of tragedy in his life that humbles him (i.e. Death in the family, a bad break-up, loss of a job/place of residence, etc). One of the most powerful influences that drive a man towards maturity and growth is Fa*therhood.*

A mother/son relationship is the closest a man will ever come to experiencing *unconditional* love; that is until he meets his first child. When a child is born, he/she knows no one except for the people who are *there,* and that child inevitably grows to know & love those two people as their *parents.* When a man stays connected to his child, it becomes almost impossible for him to disconnect; once he feels the unconditional love his child has for him, he'll never want to let him go.

Men are capable of completely disconnecting *emotionally* while being active *sexually* with a woman, however pregnancy and the birth of a child are very emotional moments for a man. When considering the well-being of a child, it's important that the parents have an ongoing happy/healthy relationship with one another that's filled with what I call "The 7 Habits of Highly Effective Relationships" [Respect, love, trust, honesty, loyalty, support, and communication]. No matter how the two of you feel about one another *romantically*, there is a bigger picture here, and you have a moral obligation to provide the best life for your child *together*.

Being sexually active with someone you're not in an exclusive relationship/marriage with can be an extreme risk factor for a woman, and should be avoided at all costs. A man who is not connected to a woman *romantically* will not be pleased with the idea of him having to access his emotions to nurse her through pregnancy, raise a child, and love the child. The shattering of his plan to simply be *casual* with her will forever leave a bad taste in his mouth and will build resentment. This is an unhealthy space for a man to be in when considering the well-fare of the child.

The power of Love through a child can certainly change a man's mind not only about the kid, but about *himself*. Who better to blame for becoming a father than *himself*? Each day he looks at his child, it's a reminder that, "*You* are accountable for your actions, whether you'd like to admit it or not. If you don't like the position you're in, change your direction and continue to move forward". The child whom he once thought was a curse can turn into a blessing once he sees the value in fatherhood; a life changing blessing that allows him to see who he really is and where he wants to be.

There's no running away from a child who looks just like you, behaves like you, and wants to know where you are, what you're doing, or when he will see you again. Instead of running from his responsibilities, he looks his kid in the eyes and lets him know, "I love you, and I will always be here!" What started out as a young man living his life selfishly with little to no direction, stemmed a man who has now discovered a new purpose for living! When it comes to his child, he shares his time, his money, but most of all, he shares his love!

It's for this reason many men who want nothing to do with the child's mother opt never to see the child. He's *afraid* of the natural love connection that will occur between a father and *his* child, so he avoids it at all costs. A man who has decided to only have a casual relationship with a woman will not be filled with joy after hearing the announcement of a pregnancy, but instead filled with outrage, and in some cases will flee.

Being an active father in your child's life doesn't only do wonders for the child, it does wonders for *you* as a man! You have an opportunity to be an influence in someone's life; someone who will value and appreciate your contributions. Some men think having a child will slow them down or "stop their flow"; on the contrary… this child will upgrade you by encouraging you to associate with people and places with higher standards.

Instead of going to a night club, being a father might prompt a man to organize a family gathering. Instead of having a regular guys night out, a father might call up his guy friends who also have kids and make a fun filled day of socializing with old buddies and watching his kid build new friendships. Instead of going grocery shopping and buying snacks and goodies, a father might take his son to the kitchen and teach him how to make frozen ice pops with 100% juice, make homemade cookies from scratch, or how about making "Smore's" over the stove...

There's only one key ingredient to being a better father and that's simply "being a better father". With all of the fun activities a father can provide for his child, what matters most to your child is that you're *there*! Take him to a high school basketball game; he won't know whether it's the "Saint Anthony Friars" or the "L.A. Lakers" playing. All that matters to him is "My Dad took me to a basketball game"! Take him to a park and challenge him to throw a football, baseball, or a Frisbee to you, tackle him to the ground as he tries to score a touchdown, and then lie there as you describe what the clouds are shaped like. Don't just throw your kid into summer camp to keep your child busy, figure out ways to form a special *bond* with your child.

There isn't enough money in the world that you can wire into an account that could replace the one-on-one experience, interactions, and life lessons a father/son have when you're *present* in a child's life. Your child needs to know that although you and his mother are separated *physically*, you're all still connected *spiritually*. He needs to know that you are grateful to have a son, and you are grateful for the one woman who loves/cares for him unconditionally. He needs to know that you'll always be a positive role model in his life, and you'll always be there for him.

Yes, *love* the mother of your child (even if/when you're not together); this is the first woman your son will fall in love with. Show him how to treat this woman, so he'll know how to treat *all* women. A child may or may not have been a part of your diabolical plan, but nevertheless, that child is here and he's here to stay, so get used to it. Any animosity between you and the mother of your child should cease and desist for your own personal growth & development, but most importantly for your child's.

Be A Good Step Dad

My father Milton C. Bostock Sr. passed away when I was only one year old. My mother Susan R. Bostock was left widowed with five young children to raise. I'm sure the last thing my mother imagined was getting married to a man she loved, bearing five children by him and then being left to raise them all on her own. Not only did her children lose their father, but also for my mother, she lost her husband and best friend. My father lost a battle to pneumonia, and his dying wishes was for his friend Vermie D. Smith to marry my mother and be a father to his children.

Vermie honored my father's wishes and married my mother, and was a father to his children until his passing in 2011. My older siblings had recollection of my biological father, but for me, a one-year-old child, Vermie was the only father I knew. I respected him for honoring my father's dying wishes by marrying my mother and vowing to act as a father figure to my siblings and me. Him and I weren't very close, but we were much closer to one another than any of my other siblings, with the exception of my younger brother Joshua, who was his biological son. It was challenging growing up because we weren't all treated fairly; we were often treated like stepchildren.

My stepfather was a hard worker, he loved to work, was never lazy, and he always provided for us. I had no issue with the things he did, I took issue with the things that he didn't do. I never got to play fight with him, ride on his shoulders or have him spin me around. He rarely disciplined me when I did something wrong and needed the authoritative voice of a man to keep me in line. He never celebrated me for any of my academic achievements at school.

What I wanted from him the most was to have a closer relationship. I wanted to engage in conversation and activities, I wanted to see him at my recitals and basketball games, I wanted his advice on talking to girls, how to find a job, how to enroll in college, etc. I wanted him to be a Dad, but unfortunately, that day never came. I had hoped to be led into greatness by him, but over time I think he forgot that I didn't view him as merely a stepfather. For me, he was my father.

I applaud him for even considering the thought of taking on a woman with five kids, for many men would've scoffed at the idea. It's a huge responsibility and to accept it means to be patient, loving, kind, understanding and supportive of this new family. It's one thing to join a club, but it's another thing to take on an active role within the club and be a fully functioning member. A husband and a father is the head of the household, he holds the command and is expected to lead. Being a leader, no matter what scenario you're in requires passion, creativity, and discernment.

Life happens, and when it does, we have to strap up our boots, roll up our sleeves and get to work on building a better one. Sure, we would all like to start our own families and not take on anyone else's, but that's not always an option for everyone. Every day families lose brothers, sons, husbands and fathers to different battles. If there is a void in someone's life, it may just be your opportunity to come in and in fill it. You just might be the second chance that a woman needs at a husband, or the second chance that a young boy/girl needs at a father.

It doesn't take the death of a father or the absence of a father in order for you to be effective. Sometimes a child can be under the same roof as their biological father but never get the love and care that a father should give his child. All it takes is something liquid to be a father, but it takes something solid to be a Dad. Being a Dad is about paying special attention to the child, caring for the child, and being actively involved in the child's life. When you come into a child's life as a stepparent, they expect you to be several steps above their actual parent.

When I say several steps, I don't mean that you have to spoil the child or anything, but rather pay close attention to the biological father's shortcomings. Your job is to be a better man, a better husband and a better father, otherwise you'll be viewed as no different from the father they already have/had. This is where getting to know the mother comes into play; the more you know about her and her relationship with the biological father, the better you'll know what role you need to play.

You have to think long term when it comes to a woman with children. If your goal is to make it last forever, you need to understand that her children will be a significant part of her life forever. It will give you peace of mind knowing that there is a mutual love and respect amongst you, your lady and the child. It is worth it to take your time and do the necessary research to try and figure out exactly how you can be an effective new addition to the family. Once you've figured it out, you'll be ready to start playing the lead role, and remain faithful that they will follow.

It's only when you don't have a plan that things will begin to fall apart. If your goal is merely to date and sleep with the mother, you'll ruin your relationship with the child. If your goal is merely to have a relationship with the child, then that should be discussed with the mother and carried out based on agreed upon terms. Overall, you want to create a balance that works for everyone. Giving the mother and the child equal opportunity to benefit from having a relationship with you and vice versa.

Winning a child over simply takes time and research, but lucky for you, you have direct access to someone who knows more about him than anyone else, the mother. In addition, you will have considerable favor with a child simply by treating the mother with love, dignity and respect. Win over the mother and you are one step closer to winning over the child. Children are very smart, they know what true love is, and they can sense when love isn't present. So if you're not genuine and sincere in your approach with the mother or with them, that window of opportunity will swiftly close.

Your goal as a stepfather isn't about what you gain; it's about what you give. What you want from this relationship is to become a valuable source of knowledge and wisdom that the child will always seek from you. You could teach him/her how to manage money and be financially responsible, or how to study for an exam, or how to build positive relationships with other people. The fact that you're taking the time to be a part of the child's life will be enough to win their respect, finding the angle is the only challenge. They want to have a closer relationship, they want to be understood, and they want someone to care.

No matter how hard the mother tries, she will never be able to deliver a message in a way that a man would. Most often, a child looks at their mom as a nag because she cares so much. In fact she cares so much that it's sometimes overwhelming, smothering and lets be honest, quite annoying. The balance that's needed here is a gentle, logical and rational approach set forth by a man they love, respect and are willing to listen to. Sometimes a child simply needs a change of scenery, and with a mother always in the picture, sometimes those "heart to hearts" can get quite boring.

So be a man, step in, step up and take charge. Let the child know that you love them, support them and will always be there for them. Don't miss the opportunity to extend your arms and give them a hug, or listen to their problems, or help them find solutions. As a stepfather, that's exactly what you are called to do. If you weren't needed, you wouldn't have been chosen for the position.

No matter the child's relationship with his biological father, your role in the household is still significant. If the child doesn't respect you, they won't respect the relationship you have with the mother. Command respect from the beginning so you won't have to demand respect in the end. A relationship between a father and son, no matter the science behind it should be healthy and filled with love. They may or may not call you Dad, but because of the significant role you plat in their lives right now, rest assured it will be you that they call on in the future.

Discipline Your Child

One thing that I love about children is their innocence and their carefree attitude in the world. They run, they play, they eat and they sleep without worrying about the serious matters in life, as they should. If we as parents left it up to our children, they would opt to eat snacks for breakfast, lunch and dinner, stay up all night watching television, or spending lavishly on toys, video games, or whatever pleasantries that come into their creative little minds. What's worse is they will carry on this same careless behavior at school, work and into their future relationships. As parents, however it is our jobs to prepare them for the reality of the world that they soon will be stepping into.

Teaching your child discipline will not only make your life as a parent easier, but it will have a greater impact on your child's future and their relationship with the world. A child's mind is full of ideas and creativity; all they need is someone to help them focus their energy in a particular area so that they'll soon learn to master their crafts. When I was growing up I loved all sports and excelled at every sport I tried. The only problem was my parents never fully paid attention to my talent and never helped me hone in on my skills. My skills grew simply from playing in the courtyard or at the park with the neighborhood kids by my own initiative.

What I needed was some 1-on-1 coaching or a team to be a part of so that I could further enhance my skills. I needed a schedule that would hold me accountable for making it on time to practices, games, etc. I needed a crowd to showcase my skills in front of and entertain on a high-octane level. I needed a uniform that symbolized how serious I was about my craft and how dedicated I was towards my discipline. Now, I know my parents weren't very interested in sports, but it would've been great to have been pushed in a direction where I could be led by someone who was.

My mother was a very strong woman, and to this day I don't know how she managed to raise five boys and one girl. We were well mannered, respectful towards adults and we stayed in a child's place because that's what we were taught to do. We knew that if we did something outside of our home that we never would dare to do at our own home that their would be consequences. We knew better and we had no excuse to act outside of our character and embarrass our family. We were disciplined early on so that we would know how to carry ourselves later on in life.

When you're a child, you don't always appreciate the endless commands and demands of a parent, but as you put them into practice in your adult life, it's our parents that we have to thank. I remember starting back when I was only five years old, my mom would have my brothers and I doing literally everything. It made sense though, why should she do all of the work when she had all of these strong/healthy boys she could delegate the tasks to. She was training us to be better men, better brothers, and soon suitable husbands and fathers. And she didn't take it easy on us at all when it came to our chores.

My mom would have us sorting laundry, washing/drying clothes, sweeping, mopping, washing dishes, cleaning out the refrigerator, cleaning the oven, cooking and so many other tedious tasks. I thank my mother for giving us this work to do because as an adult, I can do all of those things with ease, and I don't look to a woman to do it for me. She never told us *why* she was making us do all of this work, but she knew what it would do for our character. If that's not wisdom, I don't know what is. She was aware of the impact it would later have on our lives as men, and she took the time to pay it forward.

We hated doing all of these chores, but they were extremely necessary. No matter how much we wined, cried, or complained, my mother followed through with her commands and saw to it that we got the job done. That's the kind of discipline a child needs; a child doesn't need you to be their best friend. A child needs you to be their best parent. They look up to you for protection, guidance, discipline and love and as their parent, you should not want to disappoint.

No matter how old your child gets, you will always be his father. Don't ever think that because you wear the same sized clothes, are old enough to partake in the same activities, and share common interests that you are equals. There needs to be a certain level of respect and reverence between you and your child to forever ingrain in their minds that you are the father, and they are the child. A classic example of a lack of reverence is the popular animation *The Simpsons*, Bart refers to his father by his first name *Homer*. The lack of respect is reciprocal as we constantly see Homer strangling Bart anytime he feels offended by his son.

There's nothing wrong with hanging out with your child as adults, just so long as they *still* know their place. Their place is to remember who you are to them and who they are to you, and to never do anything to jeopardize the sanctity of that relationship. Many parents miss the opportunity to establish their position as an authoritative figure because they wait too long. A baby is learning the ways of the world long before they even come out of the womb. Once they enter into the world, their senses only grow stronger. Too often do parents allow their children to get stuck in their ways before they lay down the rules and regulations.

The sky is the limit in life, but if your child knows no boundaries, they will never reach your fullest potential. A parents' job is to make their child aware of the consequences associated with not following the rules. Being careless in the home could land them on punishment, but being careless in the real world could land them in far worse trouble. Society relies on our parenting skills to raise our children and prepare them to abide by the law. School is merely a secondary teaching source that is offered to those who wish to advance themselves.

Without discipline at home, a child literally won't know how to act, and when they don't know how to act they won't be able to adjust to different environments. This can cause esteem and confidence issues which can effect their performance at school, work and certainly in life. One of the things that happens when a child doesn't feel good about themselves is they search for ways to prove their worth. Sometimes this can result in a positive and extraordinary display of gifts & talents, and sometimes can result in a waste of gifts and talents. Every child wants to do well in life, but they need your help.

As a man, your role is extremely significant because you're in the leadership position and most children aspire to be just like their father. That puts you in a powerful position because most of your teachings will come through actions rather than words. Your child wants to study your every move and get set in a routine that they can follow. When they talk about their father, they don't want to have to make up a bogus story, no they want to be able to say "My father was a family man, worked hard everyday, provided for his family, and made time for the people he loved". When a child sees that your disciplined, they will model themselves after you.

When you have that conversation with your son about the importance of education, it will hold more weight when *you* have gotten *your* education. When you give your child advice on relationships, it will hold more weight when *you* have proven to have had success in your relationship. When you give your child advice on money management, it will have more credibility when *you* have managed your accounts properly and have the means to show for it. When you instruct your child that reading is fundamental, it will help if *you* can be seen engaging in new reading material on a regular basis. Pulling the "I'm your father, do what I say" card is easy; lets put that card away and start using "Follow the leader".

The goal is to make your child better than you could ever be. A great start would be to aspire to be more than the man you currently are so that your child will constantly aim higher and work harder to achieve their goals. My son Ethan melts my heart when he speaks to other people about me; he's so innocent, so honest and transparent, and that could make or break a parent. I'm sure you can recall a time in your life when your mom or dad said "Don't go telling our family business". Instead, I try and teach my son the power of words, how to use them and how to deliver a message in as few words as possible.

I don't expect my son to be anything like me, no I expect my son to be far greater. I didn't have a father who taught me things, pushed me to the limit, and provided me with the resources I needed to excel. I didn't have a father who I had to answer to when I got myself into trouble at school. I didn't have a father to check my homework, help improve my reading or public speaking abilities. I didn't have a father who hoped for the best for me and exhausted every resource in his power to help me reach the next level. But Ethan has that and he has a father who won't allow him to make any excuses for being anything but great!

Your son will get tired of you giving them instructions, tired of you pushing them in different directions, and tired of you making executive decisions, but you know better. He will get tired of reading, tired of writing, tired of speaking, tired of dancing, and tiring of performing, but you know better. He will get tired of being denied access to his friends, tired of not being allowed to play video games, and tired of being denied junk food, but you know better. He will get tired of you dragging him to church, tired of you not allowing him to party, and tired of you and your network of industry professionals, but you know better.

For many, it takes years to truly appreciate everything a parent has done for their child, but the day will come. After training up a child, you have to learn to let go and let them find their own way. Trust that all of the morals, values and principles that you've instilled in them since birth with forever be in their hearts, minds and spirits. Everything they do will be a reflection of you and everything you stand for. Use your position as a parent to discipline your child and build up strong men and women who will too inspire growth and change in the world.

The proof of your success as a parent will come when your child has become a fully functioning member of society. After seeing your son in action, you can stand proud knowing that your efforts did not go to waste. He will practice firm leadership and treat everyone with love, dignity and respect as his father has done with him. He will manage money properly, be charitable and spend wisely as his father once did in his household. He will show extreme discipline and focus in his fields of expertise and excel just as his father did in school, work and in life. Disciplining your child starts with you.

Spend Quality Time With Your Children

Being a father has got to be the most rewarding thing a man could ever experience. I was 24 when my son Ethan was born and I had one year left of college. I was attending Texas Wesleyan University in Fort Worth, TX for my final semester while my son and his mother lived in New Jersey. Back then, yahoo messenger was very popular and we both had webcams so that we could see each other. He was only a few months old and didn't do much, but at the same time, everything he did seemed to fascinate me.

This was a new experience for me and I was enjoying it. I probably drove his mother crazy because I wanted to witness EVERYTHING! I remember the first time he was able to sit up in his high chair and eat baby food, his mom used her phone to record a video of it and sent it to me. It was so funny to me because as she fed him, it was as if his mouth never closed, he was always looking for his next bite. I couldn't wait to see him again, hold him, hug him, kiss him and just spend quality time with him.

Her family and friends were a huge blessing; they came through with so many baby items and diapers for our son to last us at least a year. Lord knows we needed it; she was on maternity leave and I was just a student not knowing what my next move was in life. I was a little afraid, but I've never been a coward or one to run away from my responsibilities. Like everything else, I was going to figure this thing out and make it work. One thing I was certain about was I was excited about being a Dad.

I would brag to my best friends about all the things I would teach my son, what he would be when he grew up, and how he would look just like me and they would laugh. I was a *proud* dad if you had ever seen one. I couldn't wait until he was old enough to talk so that we could politic together. I couldn't wait for him to be able to walk and run so that we could race together. I looked forward to teaching him how to ride a bike because that's the type of thing a father does with his son.

For the moment, I was enjoying simply watching him grow up. I was in love with this kid; he had the biggest and brightest eyes, just like I did when I was a baby. He had the fattest cheeks in the world and I couldn't stop kissing and squeezing them. Once he learned how to crawl, I knew how to get him to come to me; all I had to do was show him some food. Oh yes, he loved to snack, just like his father, and I enjoyed every bit of his company.

The first few months of a newborn's life, doctors warn not to allow the child to sleep in the same bed with the parents. It's been said to be dangerous, as the parent could roll over on the child and smother him. That warning should've been given to the babies too. When he finally was big enough to sleep outside of his crib, he would somehow find his way to my face, and fall asleep right on my face. I would wake up and couldn't see a thing, nostrils covered up, and by the grace of God he left me room to breathe out of my mouth.

Initially, I would wake up alarmed, but over time I had gotten used to it and would just wake up with a smile. I knew it was my son simply trying to get closer to his dad. It was a very warm feeling to wake up to someone who loves you that much and I wouldn't trade it for the world. As I start to wake up and move, he would do the same, and the next thing you know, we're smiling and playing with one another. Then the next phase was finding something to eat; typical "men" I know. Lol

I pity those men who walk out on their children, because they are truly missing out on their blessing. It may be scary to take on such a huge responsibility, but such is life. It's not easy for the mother of your child to raise a son, and it will be that much more difficult without you. Not only does it impact their lives financially, but also emotionally and psychologically. These few memories that I've shared about my relationship with my son are priceless. These are precious times that I can share, and so can my son.

Unfortunately for many children and many fathers, they don't have positive, uplifting memories to reflect on because they didn't create any. It doesn't take a lot for you to build a relationship with your child and build a legacy, but it does require you to *be* there. Being there means that you are actively involved, attentive and aware of what's going on with your child. Not only that, but also you are participating in the activities with your child.

Throughout the week, my son is at school for most of the day, and I am at work, so when the weekends come, I make it a habit not to do any work and focus solely on spending quality time with my son. The work that I do can be very demanding and my son can also be very demanding. When I'm working, I want to give my clients my full and undivided attention, and when I'm writing I need to be focused. When I'm with my son, I need to make sure that he's safe, fed and entertained. It's kind of hard to talk on the phone with a client and make sure that my son is playing "rock, paper, scissors" with integrity. lol

To make sure that my son gets my full and undivided attention, I simply give it to him. No phone calls about work on the weekend, no emails, texts, nothing! We're too busy at church, at the park, bike riding, at home wrestling and having a good time with one another. He's had a long and tiring week at school, I've had a long and tiring week at work, so now it's time for us boys to just chill. When we go to the park, I encourage him to play with the other kids, because he's not going to wear me out. Lol But when he wants me to get involved, I gladly oblige.

Sometimes when I go to the park with my son, I see other parents constantly texting, constantly on the phone and not at all engaged with their child. All the while, the child is begging for their attention, "Look at me Daddy" as he replies "I'm looking" while still texting. I think to myself "Poor kid". Our kids look up to us, so you can look forward to them constantly trying to win your approval. They may ask you a thousand times to look at them as they prepare to do the most ordinary cartwheel in the world, but it's not about the cartwheel, it's about your attention. They want you to pay attention to them and spend quality time with them.

If a child can know the difference between spending quality time and just being around each other, you should too. You've been a child before, and you know firsthand what it was like to feel neglected, we all have. You've lived longer, so you should have more resources to provide a variety of ways to engage as a family. You don't have to wait on the mother of the child to brainstorm ideas; sometimes it's good to simply connect one on one with your child. This gives you the opportunity to show *your* creativity and value as a father.

It's easy to join a gym and stick your kid in child watch for 2-3 hours, but don't forget to make time to spend *together*. Sending them off to summer camp is great; it builds character and helps them become more sociable, but also figure out ways to create summer adventures *together*. There's nothing to sending your child off to spend the weekend at a friends house, but try hosting a sleepover of your own for your kid. The idea is to figure out ways to actually engage *with* your child as opposed to simply keeping them busy. Every child wants to have "hands on" parents who are present and also active in their activities.

After a certain age, your child simply will *stop* asking you to be a part of their lives and inwardly they'll wish you would just *be* there. That's what a father does; he is there for his child because it's *his* child. He marks his calendar when his child tells him about a performance coming up at school. He cheers him on as he does his best on and off the court, field or stage. He encourages his child to partake in extracurricular activities and practices with him at home.

It doesn't take much to receive credit for being a father, but you have to play a significant role in a child's life to be considered a dad. Your son might not remember every toy you bought him, but he will remember all the time you spent with him. He will carry these family values with him when he has his first child, and hopefully it will trickle down to his grandchildren. By spending quality time with your son, you build his character; boost his esteem and his confidence. Spend quality time with your son; he needs you now more than ever.

Support Your Child

The first thing that comes to mind when most men hear the words child support is *payments*. According to the courts, that's all child support means to *them*. They're not concerned with whether or not you are spending time with your child; all that matters to them is that you are funding the child. While providing the financial means for your child is important, he primarily needs your love. No matter how much money or gifts you give your child, what your child will value the most is your time.

I became a father at age 24, and I was so excited about opening up this new chapter in my life. I had just gotten new photography equipment and my son was the perfect subject to practice on. I've taken so many pictures of him that he (now seven years old) has developed his own love for photography. It was a great experience spending time with my son, capturing his image, and mastering my craft. I had the opportunity to learn new things as a photographer and as a father, and I was blessed to have the opportunity to teach him as well.

There was a time where he was unable to lift himself up or roll over on his own in his crib, so he would simply wine or cry until someone came to get him. This was my newborn son, so naturally I was more than happy to run to his aid and cater to his every need. I would smile at him and he would smile back, he would drink his bottle, burp and then relax quietly before falling asleep. I can't say that I enjoyed changed diapers, but it was a part of my duty as a father, and so I obliged. I remember the endless warming of the bottles; it was like all this kid ever does is eat!

As my son grew, so did his needs; bigger diapers, bigger clothes, and bigger appetite. My son was a chunky baby and I loved it. His vision was getting clearer, he know who his Mommy and Daddy was as our bonds grew stronger. He looked just like me, so there was no denying him, and we loved each other so much that if I ever left, he *himself* would probably hunt me down and find me. Abandoning my son was never a thought that crossed my mind; no matter how unprepared I was to be a father. He grew on me just as I knew he would and the feelings were mutual.

Less than a month after he turned 2 his mother and I had grown apart and we went our separate ways. I was 26, hurt from the break-up, looking for work and still trying to find myself as a man. I allowed myself to sulk for about two weeks before snapping out of it and realizing that my son needs me now more than ever. He was used to seeing me every morning and every night, and now for two weeks, I'm nowhere to be found. "I can't stop being a father just because I'm no longer with the mother" is what was going through my mind.

At this tender young age, he wasn't much of a conversationalist over the phone. In person, however he was all smiles, all fun, all games and would even talk to me as best he could because he saw me in real time. The most he would do with a phone at 2 years old is look at it, lick on it, or breath in it. We needed to connect with each other in person the way a father and son should. He wasn't aware of what was going on with his mother and I; all he cared about was being loved.

It's a simple request if you ask me; what child wouldn't want to be loved by both of their parents? I owed it to him to give him the love and support that was required of me. My son would stay with me on the weekends, and we would do father and son things like talk, go to the park and play, go to church, do arts and crafts, read, you name it. He was getting bigger and bigger and to me that meant he needed more clothes, more food, and more of my love and attention. As his father, it was my duty to provide these things without having to be asked to.

Sometimes in life, things don't always work out the way we want them to, and we're left with the mess we've created. As with any other scenario in life, you have to be able to rise to the occasion. Your responsibility as a father doesn't end when the relationship with the mother does, it ends when life itself come to a conclusion. Even if the two of you are separated physically, you must remain together spiritually for the sake of the child. A father doesn't abandon his child; he raises his child and supports them in whatever way possible.

When we make the choice to lay down with a woman and bring forth life, we must also accept the responsibility of being there for them. Too often are women left to raise children on their own that they didn't make on their own. What could possibly be more important than your offspring living in a fatherless world? As an able bodied man, you have every tool necessary to be a provider for your family. If you are in the land of the living, you still have time to spend with your children.

At this point in life, you can't afford to fall short, go to prison or worst die on your kids when they need you the most. They need your encouragement, your guidance, your protection and your love. You won't be the first man to reach a point in his life where he feels lost, but through it all, you must find your way. You must break the cycle that shows our sons and daughters that it's ok to be irresponsible and abandon your children. Show them that no matter what you are going through, you will be there for them.

Not only will this decision change your life and make you feel better as a man, but also you will regain the respect of your children and their mother. She may not ever *tell* you that she wants you to be the best man or best father you can be, but deep down inside that's what she's hoping and praying for. You may feel as though you're in this alone, but your children love you and are still looking up to you. It does neither party any good to see you doing bad, so be encouraged and know that you are expected to come out victorious. So put on your big boy pants, roll up your sleeves and take care of your business.

You won't be the first or the last man to experience a break-up that involves kids, so don't go losing your mind over it. Now is the time to regroup, get your emotions in check, keep your composure and get your finances in order. After all, that's a part of being a man anyway; you don't need a woman or a child to do this.

The first thing you need to ask yourself is "What's in the best interest of the child?" The next thing you to ask yourself is "How I am I going to make it happen?" Once you've thought of a plan and have spoken it into existence, take action and make it a reality.

The term "Deadbeat Dad" isn't something that women are making up; this is a reality for them. A man comes into their lives, knocks them up and then for whatever reason doesn't feel the immediate need or sense of urgency to provide for the child. Now it's one thing for you to not be supportive physically and emotionally, but to not be supportive financially in addition to that further reduces your credibility as a man. *We* are the protectors and the providers, it's our role. If you're not doing either, then you are failing yourself as a father and as a man.

Your child doesn't simply *want* you to be a part of their lives; they *need* you to be. As they grow older, so will their needs. I remember when my son Ethan was in pre-k, it was his first Holiday play and he wanted me to be there. On the day of, I snuck into the room where they were performing with my camera in hand and found a good spot. As they were getting ready to perform, Ethan would look all across the room to see if I had finally arrived. I would wave at him to let him know where I was standing and he would have the biggest smile on his face.

He was so proud and so happy to see me; he would tell all of his teachers and friends "look, that's my Daddy, over there look". The whole time he would look in my direction and smile as he sang the songs he had memorized, and after it was over he'd run and jump into my arms. As a father, *these* are the moments I look forward to, the moments where I get to witness my son performing in life. I don't cry often, but on *that* day when I saw how happy my presence made my son, I cried tears of joy. It motivated me to do whatever I needed to do as a man, to make myself readily available and accessible to my son as a father.

You won't know much of a difference your support will make in your child's life until you give it. You won't know how happy you can possibly make your child until you see it. You won't be able to experience the rewards of being a father until you do it. Having a child is truly a blessing, but you must also remember that *you* are your child's blessing. Continue to love, protect, provide and support your child for all the days of your life. Step up and be the Dad your child needs you to be.

50 Motivational Quotes From Cheyenne Bostock

If you want a woman to respect you as the man of the house, you need to be adding value to the house.

A woman wants a man who offers security; someone who can love, protect and provide on a consistent basis. And be loyal!

Excuses are for the useless. Opportunity is everywhere! Be proactive!

If you need a female friend outside of your relationship/marriage, you've committed to the wrong woman!

If you are unemployed, your 9-5 should be finding a 9-5.

You will attract more women when you focus on your goals and stop thinking about attracting more women.

All it takes is a little liquid to be a Father. It takes something solid to be a Dad.

All a woman wants is for you to have a plan! No woman wants to follow a man who isn't a leader!

Take a woman for a walk in the park, listen, ask questions, make eye contact, and keep hands off. It will be the best date she ever had!

Worthy women usually aren't easy women!

A woman needs to feel comfortable before allowing a man to be intimate with her. Always remember that sex depends on "her" mood.

When it comes to meeting/dating women, it's important to take your time. If you rush the process, you won't see much progress.

Find out what a woman's interests are and then use that information to spark conversation and create future opportunities to connect.

Being broke is no excuse not to get creative and take your lady out on dates.

If God is not in your relationship, you shouldn't be either.

A woman will leave you emotionally long before she leaves you physically. You might still *see* her, but you will no longer have her.

You can get any woman in the world if you know what to say. You can keep any woman if you know what to do.

Your woman should be your one and only female friend. #Loyalty

You are the head of the household. Not to be confused with the "boss". Your job as the head is to lead, protect and provide.

People tell lies to avoid losing someone or something. People tell the truth to avoid losing themselves. #Integrity #Character

Cheating is any welcomed and/or initiated interaction (outside of your relationship) w/someone you know is romantically interested in you.

A "break-up" means "no more access". You haven't truly broken up if you are still connected.

Putting your hands on a woman shows how weak you are. Walking away shows how strong you are.

Respect women for no other reason than the fact that she's a woman. #Integrity

Don't expect her to be a housewife if you're not a providing husband.

She should already possess qualities/characteristics of a wife long before you marry her.

Your past isn't who you are; it's who you were. Who you are is the person you've become *after* experiencing your past. #Growth

Your past will never be the present! It's never too late to reinvent yourself!

Even when times get hard, the road gets rough and it seems as though nobody cares... Never give up!

Live right. Worry less!

It's easier to make decisions when it comes to the heart, when you have discernment. If you are not led by God, you'll be lost in the world.

Before you set out to reach your goals, know that success and great results don't and won't come easy. Be ready to work!

The fastest way to eliminate a problem is to address it.

Just because a person appears to be doing well doesn't mean they don't need love, support and encouragement.

Stop getting intimidated by people who are doing better than you. Start getting motivated!

Don't be afraid to let go of people just because you've known them for years. If there's been no growth in years... It's time!

Sometimes you have to let old relationships die in order for your new relationship to live.

It's impossible to have a spouse and a friend of the opposite sex and be loyal to both at the same time.

Your "Purpose" is the thing God called you to do before your time is up.

If you want to be popular, say what people want to hear. If you want to change the world, say what people don't.

You can learn all about a person's character not by what they plan to do, but by what they've already done.

Your *Character* is the decisions you make with the time you've been given.

Stop trying to convince the world that you've changed. Start showing the world that you've learned and you've grown!

You can't build a successful business or relationship w/others if you are not willing to be transparent about whom you are/where you've been.

Stay focused, set goals, have a plan, take action, serve your community, connect with other people, change lives. Form a business plan.

Safe sex is getting married and being loyal!

Low self-esteem is simply a result of a person not knowing and/or believing in the calling that God has on their life. #Purpose

Most people won't believe in your greatness until you show them. Let your work speak for itself.

Giving is about what you put forth, not what you get back.

If the foundation of your relationship isn't love, your relationship will eventually crumble.

If you want a woman to stay, give her hope. If you want a woman to leave, give her doubt.

A woman loves it when you are always busy taking care of your business, but never too busy for her.

Bio

Cheyenne Bostock is a Life & Relationship Expert, motivational speaker and best selling author of Food, Sex & Peace Of Mind. He is one of media's go-to sources for real and uncut advice on life, love and relationships. His work has been featured in a variety of national and international media outlets including newspapers, magazines, radio and television. He is a regular on The Bill Cunningham Show, and has been featured on Fox News, Chasing NJ, News 12 BK, Arise TV, and Fusion TV. For more info, follow @AskCheyB and visit www.askcheyb.com. For bookings, contact Buffy: (646) 389-7145, email info@askcheyb.com

www.ingramcontent.com/pod-product-compliance
Lightning Source LLC
LaVergne TN
LVHW041612070426
835507LV00008B/202